THE GARDEN POOL

THE
GARDEN
POOL

FRANCES PERRY
MBE FLS

South Brunswick and New York
GREAT ALBION BOOKS

First American edition published 1972
by Great Albion Books, a division of
Pierce Book Company, Inc., Cranbury,
New Jersey 08512

Library of Congress Catalogue Card Number 70-181503

ISBN 0-8453-1091-7

Printed in Great Britain

Contents

List of Illustrations

8   LIST OF ILLUSTRATIONS

CHAPTER I

Water in the Garden

MANY thousands of new pools appear in British gardens each season—small ones, large ones; formal and informal; raised above the ground or artfully sunk below the level of the surrounding soil.

They are made from a miscellany of materials such as concrete, prefabricated fibreglass, plastic sheeting, plastolene liners, puddled clay, even old bath tubs, cisterns and sawn-down casks, for any receptacle which holds water is a potential water garden.

The reasons for their popularity are not difficult to appreciate. Water has a fascination for both the young and the old, as is evidenced by the way children like to make mud pies and adults flock to the coast and rivers for recreational pursuits.

In a garden water has many attractions, which is why the world's landscape architects use it so frequently in their designs. It has a magnetic quality which draws birds, animals and people. The purling stream, cascading waterfall and playing fountain are themselves indicative of life and movement, and there is music in their different notes—from the low murmuring or rippling treble of the sluggish stream to the heavy splash of a high waterfall. Aquatic features soften the hard contours of adjacent buildings and give a sense of spaciousness to the smallest garden. Still water duplicates neighbouring trees and plants in its mirrored surface and also reflects the mood of the elements— the dancing raindrops, gloomy rain clouds or sparkling sunshine.

In addition the possession of water enables us to grow many beautiful and uncommon plants which would not succeed anywhere else in the garden. During a hot dry summer it creates a restful effect and drowsing beside the pool one can watch brightly coloured fish sporting in its depths, enjoy the song of visiting birds and experience a peace which justifiies all the labours of construction.

Whatever type of water garden is envisaged it is important to site it in an open position exposed to full sunshine. Ponds under trees or in dark corners are rarely inspiring. They have a gloomy look, are often cloudy because of rotting leaves, sometimes smell offensively and invariably the water plants fail to show much bloom.

The question of light also applies to pools under glass— as in a greenhouse or sunlounge. Unless there is toplight (natural or artificial) the plants grow weak and leggy and only bloom spasmodically.

STREAM GARDENS

Few gardens are blessed with natural water, but where it exists the most satisfactory effects are achieved by embodying it in an informal landscape design. The flow is unlikely to be straight and any bends and curves should be preserved as this achieves a natural appearance. Damming and diverting may be resorted to if it seems necessary to achieve these aims.

If the stream flows through and beyond the garden it may

be wise to leave it that way. Interference with natural water can cause flooding at the rear or the cutting off of supplies in front—either of which may annoy neighbours.

A very small stream however, or one likely to dry out in summer may sometimes be improved by allowing the surplus water (in its season) to wend its way into a large pool. Where it occurs on a clay subsoil puddling may render the pond watertight, but usually it will have to be lined with plastic sheeting or concrete. In dry weather, when natural water has to be augmented by artificial means a tap at the top end of the garden will prove useful. Alternatively there are special pumps sold for the purpose of returning water from a low to high level, so that it can be used over and over again.

A stream can be made the focal point of a garden, with waterfalls, pools and cascades. Expense is usually the deciding factor with such developments, and labour prices and the cost of water, rocks and plants should be looked at before embarking on very elaborate schemes. However, even in a simple way meandering slowly on its course, the natural charms of a stream may be enhanced by planting the banks with irises, water forget-me-nots, kingcups and similar moisture-loving plants, while the use of stepping stones will check its flow if desired.

Where practicable the marshy ground around should be top-dressed with a good layer of loam, peat and sand to take irises, day-lilies, primulas and other plants which thrive on damp—as opposed to wet—soil.

Stream effects can also be achieved artificially, and look particularly well planned in association with a rock garden. The water should be introduced at the highest point and allowed to fall over rocks and run through narrow verges to a larger pool at a lower level. Here again, taps and pumps should be installed to return the water.

A stream can often be achieved artificially in the rock garden

It is important not to make the falls and streams perfectly straight. Water always takes the line of least resistance and in nature seeks out the softest and easiest paths so that its descent (or course) is winding. These irregularities should be copied in an artificial stream. Falls, rills and pools may be constructed with the aid of polythene sheeting—previous excavations being lined with this material—with the edges tucked beneath soil or rocks, to disguise its artificial nature.

Such features can also be constructed of concrete, or garden sundriesmen sell tough resin-bonded glassfibre shapes (pools, waterfalls and narrow channelled sections to simulate streams), which can be linked at different levels to make a complete stream garden. Although light to handle and easy to install the latter (particularly the waterfalls) are rarely as pleasing to look at as those of concrete or polythene sheeting. They are also more expensive.

Rock interspersed with plants and water provides most pleasing effects. Grey weathered limestone is especially attractive but red sandstone, tufa or even grey granite can be used. Transport costs may prove the deciding factor and local material (when available) will probably be the least costly. It pays to shop around before purchase and to remember that a few large pieces of stone are often more effective than many small pieces.

FORMAL POOLS

Formal pools call for quite different treatment. They are man-made in an artificial setting and no attempt should be made to disguise the fact. Whatever their shape—square, circular, longitudinal or stylised—they should fit in with the surrounding features.

This point is often overlooked in practice, with the result that the pond looks neither one thing nor the other. One does not put a square bed of tulips in the middle of a rock garden—such features are kept to a formal setting. Similarly with the formal pool, its tailored outline calls for bold treatment such as a broad edging of flagstones, also space around so that it becomes a dominant feature.

A formal pool can be sunk in the soil to ground level or raised above its surroundings or made flush against a building. In every case the edges should be prominent and bold with broad paths around so that approach is easy. Overplanting is a common fault and two thirds of the water should be left clear of vegetation. Use low growing aquatics such as water-lilies, water hawthorns, submerged oxygena-

An attractive sunken pool. Concrete slabs or paving stones
will hide any irregularities in the walls

tors and the occasional water iris to break the flatness. Tall
reeds are undesirable as they increase very rapidly and soon
give the pool a cluttered appearance.

The formal pool is the only type in which to place fountains.

FOR ROOF GARDENS OR VERY SMALL AREAS

Prefabricated resin-bonded glassfibre pools are ideal for
small areas and their installation is simple. Some have
punched out planting pockets which allow for different
depths of water; others are approximately the same depth
all over in which case the aquatics are planted in pots and
then stood in position.

To install a prefabricated pool excavate a hole a little larger than seems necessary, set the pool in place and test it for levels (it will annoy you for years if the water runs to one end). Then pack it round, first with sand or fine soil and finally the rest of the excavated material.

Finally bed some paving stones on sand round the edges to give it some prominence, plant and fill with water. Prefabricated pools can also be used on roof gardens or in a sun lounge, only in this case they must be supported with brick or concrete so that they stand firmly on the ground.

Sawn down beer or wine casks make excellent small pools —either free standing or sunk into soil. They should be reduced to about 18in and have an initial washing. Six inches of compost should then be placed over the base, a water-lily planted in the centre and one or two other aquatics and then filled with water. These tubs must be kept topped up, otherwise the staves shrink and they start to leak.

When several tubs are sunk into the ground quite pretty effects can be achieved by planting low-growing bog plants between—keeping these moist in dry weather by allowing the tubs to occasionally overflow.

Baths, sinks, old coppers and cisterns can all be brought into use in the water garden, although some metals— notably zinc and lead—sometimes adversely affect fish.

CHAPTER II

Concrete and Plastic for Pool Making

THE main materials used today as pool liners are concrete and plastic, depending on the size of the pool, the wear and tear to which it is likely to be subjected and how much one wishes to spend.

Concrete pools are the most durable and easier than plastic to empty for replanting purposes but they take longer to make, are more expensive to install and call for a considerable amount of hard constructional work. They are also very difficult to remove—should this ever become necessary—and mending leaks is more tedious than replacing or repairing a plastic liner.

PLASTIC LINERS

In recent years polythene has largely replaced concrete as a medium for lining home garden pools. It is light to handle and easy to manipulate; even a novice can use it with confidence.

However ordinary polythene sheeting is too flimsy for most containers, although 500 or 1000 gauge material (used double) may be serviceable enough for lining rock pools or as a temporary measure. In most cases it pays to purchase the thicker, stronger materials, especially the PVC sheeting known as juralene, or the terylene reinforced plastolene. These are really tough and will last years unless damaged with sharp tools or rocks.

Calculating the quantity of sheeting material required for a specific pool is worked out as follows. The length required will be the overall length of the pool plus twice its maximum depth; and the width the overall width of the pool plus twice its maximum depth. No allowance is made for turn over at the edges as the material stretches when filled with water and leaves ample spare for tuck ins at the margins.

Plastic pools must always be kept full of water because weathering—particularly strong sunlight—can damage the fabric and cause it to leak. Sharp tools should be used with caution near them, although the thicker fabrics (but not polythene) can be repaired with a patch of the same material and a good adhesive. When undertaking patching make sure that both pool and patch are bone dry and clean.

CONCRETE POOLS

There are still people who prefer concrete for pool making and for those built above ground level it is essential. The material is strong, lasts many years and gives great scope for variations in shape and use.

It is important to mix the ingredients carefully and have a strong cement base; economies may result in porosity and leakage. A common formula is 3 parts crushed, clean, loam-free aggregate (varying in size from $\frac{3}{16}$ to $\frac{1}{4}$in) 2 parts clean sand and 1 part cement. Work should commence on the floor of the pool and then the sides. Some firms sell pre-mixed concrete which saves much hard work, but it has to

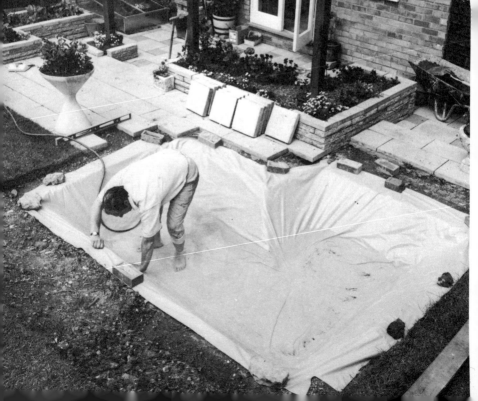

Three stages in constructing a plastolene pool. (*Above left*) excavating the pool; (*below left*) stretching the plastic by filling the pool with water; (*above*) laying paving round the edges to keep the plastic in position, and to protect the pool edge

be used quickly, so that extra labour may be necessary to expedite the job. Concrete starts to set in twenty minutes so that time is *not* on the side of the worker.

Anyone contemplating making a concrete pool would be well advised to consult the Cement and Concrete Market ing Association bulletin (No. 38.002) *Concrete in Garden Making*. This deals with all aspects of pool making.

In any case concrete pools are best constructed in the autumn and should be kept filled with water all winter. This gives them several months test against leakage and a period during which the free lime (always present in new concrete) may seep out into the water. This lime can injure fish and plants and must be got rid of, but if the pool is emptied and rinsed in spring it should be ready for imme- diate planting.

There is no need to excavate any garden pool deeper than 2ft 6in. This allows for 6in concrete, 6in of compost (or the depth of a water-lily basket) and 18in of water. Few hardy water-lilies need more than 18in of water above their crowns and this depth is sufficient to prevent a complete freeze through in winter. Shallow pockets—to take marg- inal aquatics—or a deep section for the benefit of the fish in hot weather can be constructed as the work proceeds.

Large concrete pools may need some form of reinforce- ment and a plug or outlet may be convenient when the pond has to be emptied. Full details concerning methods are given in the bulletin, which can be obtained from 52 Grosvenor Gardens, London, S.W.1.

CHAPTER III

Composts and Planting

ONE of the great advantages with aquatics is that there is no
need to worry about sun, winds or droughts affecting them,
nor is there any necessity to stake or protect freshly moved
plants. The one necessary precaution is to defer transplant-
ing until the weather becomes warm and settled. Consequently it is usual to postpone lifting hardy water-lilies
until about mid-April or May, when growth is just commencing and the shock of the operation causes little set-
back. The season extends until about mid-June, when it is
wise to stop, for the plants are then growing vigorously and
may not have sufficient growing period left (especially in a
dull summer) in which to recover from the move. This rule
goes for most of the heavily rooted aquatics—aponogetons,
nuphars, pontederias, etc.—but the lesser water plants and
submerged oxygenators have a longer season. They may be
moved at almost any time during the growing season, and
in the aquarium even throughout the winter months.

COMPOSTS

Water-lilies are gross feeders and need a rich soil, rather
on the heavy side. I have seen them in natural ponds grow-

ing magnificently in almost pure clay; the strong white roots thrust down so far that they were almost impossible to lift without severing most of them. I knew a man once who made after considerable labour a fine clay pond and in it placed some water-lilies growing in baskets. In course of time the lilies grew too big and in taking up the basket remains he broke a number of roots, which had penetrated right through to the clay base. These eventually died and withered and the pond began to leak. To cut a long story short, it was later found that the roots had penetrated so deeply and efficiently as to make the pond quite porous in these parts. Obviously the lily roots had a penchant for clay.

The water gardener uses heavy loam, which is more manageable than clay, and enriches it with cow-manure if possible, for this is the best of water-lily fertilisers. If arrangements can be made, it should be prepared a year in advance by making up a compost of five parts soil and one part cow manure, turned and mixed once or twice during the year. The original loam should be full of fibre and slightly greasy to the touch. During the period of stacking all organic material will disintegrate, and by the time it is wanted it will be rich and full of plant food and yet unlikely to set up fermentation when the water is added. If it is impracticable to prepare for things so far ahead, use loam (coarsely screened and with the fibre removed) mixed with coarse bonemeal. The latter substance is used at the rate of a quart per barrowload of loam.

On no account substitute the cow manure or bonemeal with other animal manures; I have seen a whole planting of water-lilies killed after horse dung had been used. Poultry guano is too rich, and sheep, pig and rabbit manures cause fermentation and water discoloration. For the same reason avoid using peat, leaf-mould, spent hops, or any of the usual organic substitutes. Sand in the compost is not necessary: its presence in ordinary composts is designed to assist drainage—quite pointless in the water garden. Nevertheless, when fish are present in the pool they frequently cause water discoloration by stirring up the mud, and a layer of sand over the compost does prevent this— even more effective is a layer of shingle or granite chippings.

MATURING THE CONCRETE

Before any planting at all is done the gardener must be quite certain that the concrete is matured, and that no ill effects will be suffered by plants and fish. Overwintered full of water, the pool should be safe once this water has been removed and the concrete rinsed.

Very new pools can, however, be very dangerous, for the alkaline properties which emanate from fresh concrete are exceedingly toxic. To neutralise these substances fill the tank with water and add sufficient commercial syrupy phosphoric acid to show an acid reaction to litmus at two tests, at twenty-four-hour intervals. Alternatively, the whole of the tank can be painted over with a bituminous paint to seal the pores and prevent any of these substances leaking through.

Although without chemical significance, a method which quickly matures the pool consists of filling it with water and stirring in sufficient crystals of permanganate of potash to colour the liquid wine-red. After some days the liquid clears and discloses a sludge lying on the bottom. The pond should then be emptied and rinsed and is ready for planting; livestock, however, must not be introduced for another six or eight weeks.

In the case of prefabricated or plastic sheeting pools no special preparation is necessary. They are safe to plant immediately after installation.

PLANTING

There are two methods of growing lilies in artificial ponds. One is to cover the bottom with 5 to 6in of prepared compost and plant directly into it, and the other is to use containers of wood, concrete or basket. The disadvantage of the first arises when it becomes necessary to attend to the plants, for the gardener churns up the mud and the water loses its clarity.

Planting should be carried out whilst the pool is still empty, using the compost in much wetter condition than would be normal in other parts of the garden. Dry soil does not bind effectively, and once the water is added the roots come floating up. Plant the lilies correctly, according to their types; those with a rhizome should be placed horizontally and firmly set with the growing point and the top of the rhizome just protruding. The Marliacea varieties grow from a collar, with the rootstock going straight down into the ground. They must be set upright with the crown just visible.

Level off and cover the whole surface with an inch of plain loam, sand or shingle whichever is available. Oxygenators and other aquatics can be planted at the same time and when all is finished run in just enough water to cover the crowns of the lilies. After about a week—or less if the weather is very warm—run in another inch or two and continue like this until the pond is quite full, possibly six to eight weeks later. This may seem tedious, but it is definitely a worthwhile procedure. The water-lilies have already sustained one shock through being transplanted, and to aggravate this by running about 18in of cold water—usually straight from the tap—on to their un-established roots is most unwise. By running in the water in direct ratio to the growth you bring things along gradually, and are often rewarded by flowers the first season.

PLANTING IN BASKETS AND CONTAINERS

Sometimes the pool is constructed with concrete containers as an integral part of the set-up. Nearly always they are made with solid sides, which is a mistake, for not all lilies will live in this enclosed body of earth to which no air has access. The copper, orange and some of the pink sorts are particularly allergic to enclosed containers. The right receptacles have spaces left at intervals so that air and water come in contact with the roots. To prevent the soil from sifting out, the spaces can be stuffed with pieces of rotted turf or covered with wire or zinc netting.

Baskets, of course, are ideal and have the advantage that they can be moved to fresh positions or taken up for replanting. Their chief drawback is that they hold only a

Plant water-lilies very firmly in wet compost

relatively small amount of compost, and when this is exhausted the lily has to be replanted. Starvation signs are made apparent by small, yellowing leaves, meagre blooms, and a general lack of vigour. The position may be helped by applying bonemeal pills in spring. They are made by mixing a small 60 flower-pot full of bonemeal with sufficient wet clay to bind it together. This will make two round 'cannon-ball' pills—sufficient for one large or two medium-sized lilies. They should be thrust into the soil near the roots.

Plant the lilies firmly in the baskets and slide them into the water so that they rest just below the surface. This may necessitate raising them on bricks for the time being, but as growth progresses these can gradually be removed.

PLANTING IN NATURAL PONDS

If a natural pond with rich mud at the base is available the planting and cultivation of hardy water-lilies is simple indeed. All that is necessary is to obtain a dormant rhizome or tuber, tie it to a brick and drop it into the water at the place where you wish it to grow. Precautions should be taken to ensure that the selected spot is not more than 2ft to 2ft 6in deep, yet deep enough to ensure that the roots will not freeze in winter. With the exception of water-lilies, nuphars, aponogetons and other aquatics with tuberous rootstocks, most water plants thrive satisfactorily in pure loam. Manures are unnecessary, and indeed inadvisable, for many of them grow too vigorously as it is.

CLOUDINESS IN THE POND

A natural phenomenon which often causes perturbation is cloudiness and discoloration of the water soon after planting. This is caused by chemical changes resulting from biological activities of microscopic plants and animals. The upheaval often causes gaseous eruptions from the soil and the rise of scummy material to the surface. Remove the latter by drawing an old newspaper across the surface, but otherwise let well alone. Conditions will right themselves and the pond water clear in a few weeks. Chemical rectifiers give but temporary alleviation and they alter the chemical balance of the pool so that unforeseen complications may occur later.

A fact to be appreciated by everyone owning a pool is that the less it is emptied the better. Old, still water, which has become settled and balanced is something to strive for, and every time the pool is emptied the whole process has to be gone through again.

CHAPTER IV

Seasonal Care and Propagation

WINTER CARE OF PLANTS AND POOLS

WINTER precautions in the water garden are largely dependent upon the depth of the pool, its exposure, and the severity of the weather but hardy water-lilies will be alright if there is sufficient water above their crowns to prevent the roots from freezing. A hole should be kept broken in the ice and a floating log will take up the expansion and prevent injury to fish, plants and concrete. There are also water heaters available, suitable for small pools.

In very severe weather a simple way of protecting plants and fish is to allow preliminary freezing, and when the ice is about an inch thick break a hole and, with a rubber tube, siphon off about 2in of water. The remaining ice forms a cover for the pool, acting in fact like a greenhouse light. The hole in its surface can be covered with a board or sack.

Small shallow ponds can sometimes be kept from freezing by laying resinous branches of trees—such as pine or fir —across, or planks piled with straw protect plants and fish adequately. It is, however, necessary to remove this covering directly a thaw sets in; otherwise the plants may start into premature growth.

Extremely shallow pools, such as are found in rock gardens supporting the pygmy lilies, should be emptied completely in very severe weather, and the roots covered with a liberal mulch of leaves. These may be removed in early spring and the water returned. The lilies will suffer no harm, but oxygenating aquatics might, so remove these when the pool is emptied.

SPRING WORK IN THE WATER GARDEN

Spring work in the water garden entails the planting out of new water-lilies, dividing old ones, and a general over-haul of the bog plants in the vicinity. Fish, which will be feeling the after-effects of the winter fast, should be liberally fed with a good diet. Chopped earthworms, dried or live daphnia, rubbed raw meat and Bemax make a welcome variation to the everlasting biscuit meal.

A certain amount of algae will make its appearance and some discoloration of the water may occur. This is the usual indication that spring is round the corner, but, as explained in the last chapter, when left alone cloudy water in pools has a tendency to clear itself. The use of scavengers—such as snails—will help to keep down algae and thus improve water clarity, but too many can be a nuisance. For a pond measuring 6ft by 12ft three dozen is ample. The fish will prevent too rapid increase, but in cases of overstocking, lay one or two cabbage or lettuce plants in the tank overnight and remove them in the morning when clustered with snails. Daphnia will also clear a pool of algae.

Keep old flower heads removed from aquatics during the season, especially plants like alisma, typha, and *Iris pseudacorus*, or they will smother the pond in a few seasons. For the sake of appearance, yellowing and dead foliage should also be dealt with. A convenient way of doing this in deep water is to lash a knife or razor blade (cut-throat type) to a bamboo cane and cut as close to the root as possible. A net on a long handle will bring the material in afterwards and can also be used for removing the silky types of algae. The rough kinds which come away in ropes can be dealt with by thrusting a bamboo cane into the growth and twisting it; on lifting the cane the weed comes trailing behind.

The leaves of water-lilies are sensitive to insecticides, but they may be attacked by blackfly; a vigorous hosing dislodges these into the water where the fish make short work of them.

PROPAGATION : (I) DIVISION

Generally speaking, the usual way to propagate the hardy water-lilies is by means of division. The roots are lifted in spring and cut into pieces—each portion containing a growing shoot, a portion of the old tuber and a certain amount of root if possible. The latter is not absolutely essential, provided the 'eye', as it is called, is treated properly afterwards. Even very small pieces about the size of a thumbnail will grow.

The chief essentials to success are shallow water and not too much soil. Heavy loam, finely screened, and a little powdered charcoal is the best compost; the 'eyes' are put into pots, pans or boxes and just covered with water. Very small 'eyes' should be kept in a greenhouse—temperature round about 60°—until roots develop, and may be put outside about the end of June or early July.

Larger clumps may be grown outside the whole time. When dividing, remove any of the tuber which may be discoloured and take away the thick, coarse roots. These were the anchorage roots of the old plant and are not now needed; concentrate instead on the young fibrous ones which will be lying around them. Plant the tubers as recommended in the last chapter.

PROPAGATION: (II) SEED SOWING

A few hardy water-lilies may be raised from seed, but the number is limited. Most of the varieties grown today are of hybrid origin, many of them raised at the end of last century and the beginning of this by a Frenchman called Marliac. Marliac discovered the means of crossing hardy species such as *N. alba, alba rubra* and *tuberosa,* and also raised hybrids from the Mexican *Nymphaea mexicana.* The methods he used were never divulged and the secret died with him; no one has yet been able to emulate his examples on any grand scale. I remember my father-in-law telling me of a visit to Marliac just before the First World War. On being asked his hybridising methods, Marliac offered the secret for £1,000, or, he said, 'It will take you forty years to find out'. That time-limit has been reached, but the enigma—if there was one—is still unsolved.

What we do know is that certain kinds do set seed, as, for example, *N. tetragona, brackleyi rosea, odorata,* etc., and that hybridising should not be attempted in the early part of the season, since few pods mature their seeds then. It is better to wait until August, for almost infertile hybrids—as most of Marliac's forms are—if they mature pods at all, do so only in the latter part of the season. Fertilisation should take place on the day the female flower opens and this is made apparent by the appearance of the bloom. The first day the centre of the flower is filled with a sweet watery fluid, secreted by the stigma which is receptive at the time. Not until the second day from opening is the pollen ripe and liberated from the anthers. The first flower should therefore be fertilised with pollen from an older bloom. Results of all this hybridisation are usually very disappointing. In some respects there are too many cultivars, but we could do with some blue hardy lilies and more pygmies and doubles.

If seed is obtained it must be kept moist and cold until sown. Sow in shallow pans of screened loam and charcoal and lightly cover the seeds with sand. Submerge the pans just under water and stand in a house—temperature about 60°—and as soon as the first true leaves appear the seedlings should be transplanted to pots or boxes.

Most of the hardy aquatics with fibrous or running rootstocks can be propagated by division in spring and planted straight into their permanent quarters. Seeds should always be sown in the method advocated for water-lilies. Some plants are increased by soft cuttings; most of the submerged oxygenators are raised in this way, chiefly during the spring and summer. Young, growing pieces, several inches long, are removed from the plant, and dibbled into deep pans containing an inch or two of loam and sand, and kept filled with water. They root more rapidly in a temperature round about 60°. Methods of increasing individual plants are given in the appropriate sections dealing with their cultivation.

CHAPTER V

Hardy Water-lilies

No one will quarrel with the assertion that the water-lily holds pride of place amongst aquatics, for few plants have aroused such universal admiration or can lay claim to a more historical background. Being indigenous to most countries of the world, it was well known to primitive man, who, groping in the darkness for signs and portents of the Deity who made him, saw in this bloom a living symbol of regeneration and purification. Did it not rise pure and undefiled from the mud and slime of the river, and were not its perennial habits symbolic of life and immortality as well as resurrection?

A Chinese writer of the second century writes: 'Since the opening days of the T'ang Dynasty (A.D. 600) it has been fashionable to admire the paeony; but my favourite is the water-lily. How stainless it rises from its slimy bed, how modestly it reposes on the clear pool—an emblem of purity and truth! Symmetrically perfect, its subtle perfume is wafted far and wide, while there it rests in spotless state, something to be regarded reverently from a distance, and not to be profaned by familiar approach.' The Chinese water-lily is *Nymphaea tetragona,* a white-flowered pygmy which throws many forms and has an extensive geographical range in Asia, Australia, America, and eastern Europe.

Botanically the water-lily, or *Nymphaea* as it is known, is closely related to the buttercup and magnolia, and is believed to form a connecting link between the flowering plants and the cycads (seed-bearing palms) of prehistoric times. Through the ages, and by a process of natural selection, the species we know today have evolved, but examination of fossil plants indicates that great climatic changes have taken place in some areas. As an example of this, the presence of fossil tropical species in eastern Europe lead one to assume that the temperatures in these areas were at one time very much warmer than they are today.

Water-lilies hold pride of place among aquatic plants

Although the water-lily has interested many primitive
peoples, it is its association with the ancient Egyptians that
has excited popular attention. As the Lotus of the Nile the
water-lily played an important part from the Fourth Dynasty (about 4000 B.C.), especially in religious observances.
Offerings of blooms were made to the dead or placed on the
altars before the gods.

Schweinfurth found petals of the white *N. lotus* and the
blue *N. caerulea* in the funeral wreaths of Rameses II
(1580 B.C.) and Amenhotep I. The flower was portrayed
in the mural decorations of the time, and on the furniture,
pottery and other objects associated with their daily lives. It
is possible that the reference in Kings i. 26 to the pillars of
King Solomon's Temple, 'and it was an hand's breadth
thick, and the brim thereof was wrought like the brim of a
cup with flowers of lilies', refers to water-lilies.

The blooms were cultivated extensively for temple use,
and also used in the houses. When an Egyptian nobleman
of rank entertained, slaves presented the guests on entering
with a bud or flower of the Lotus. These they were expected
to hold in their hands of wear twined in the hair. The ex-
planation is not positively understood, but it is possible that
the custom symbolised the peaceful intentions of the guests
and that the Lotus was chosen because of the esteem in
which it was held.

The use of flowers at funerals was very prevalent; the
custom being to lay wreaths on the mummy in concentric
semicircles from the chin downward until the sarcophagus
was quite packed with floral tributes. In many cases the
preservation of these has been so perfect that botanists have
been able to identify them positively. What is particularly
interesting is that they have not been able to detect the
slightest difference between these flowers and those of the
species growing there today. This means that the transmu-

tation of these plants is very slow or non-existent and, more important still, that the climatic conditions there have undergone very little change during the past 4,000 years.

Mention of the Lotus raises some question as to its identity, for two plants were known to the ancient Egyptians as Lotus—only one of which was a nymphaea. There are two water-lilies native to Egypt, one a white, broad-petalled, nocturnal bloomer called *N. lotus*, and the other, *N. caerulea*, has narrow-petalled, sky-blue flowers which open during the day. The blue-flowered form is often depicted in murals and was much cultivated, but it is conceivable that the white form was also grown on account of its sweet scent and night-blooming qualities.

The other plant known as Lotus was *Nelumbo nucifera*, an Asiatic aquatic which has interesting associations with Buddhism. It is thought to have been introduced to Egypt about the time of the Persian invasion (525 B.C.) and much planted by the Nile because of its edible qualities. This is the plant that Herodotus speaks of as the 'rose lily of the Nile' with 'fruit like a wasp's nest' and edible seeds 'of the size of an olive stone'. The Egyptians ground the seeds down to a powder and, using this as flour, mixed it with milk and water to make loaves. The fact that they thus made bread from the plant and propagated it by wrapping each seed in a ball of clay and throwing it into the Nile, is thought to be referred to in the Bible, when we read: 'Cast thy bread upon the waters, for thou shalt find it after many days'.

The belief that this Lotus (Nelumbo) was introduced by artificial means is strengthened by the fact that it has entirely disappeared from modern Egypt.

Since earliest times water-lilies have had economic uses, the seeds and tubers being used for food and the leaves and flowers medicinally. The tubers of *N. alba* have been employed for dyeing in Ireland and Scotland and in the making of beer in France.

We find, too, that the water-lily has such grace and beauty that Indian poets have compared almost every part of the human body to it at some time or other. It has been deemed worthy offering to the gods, and fitting symbol of civilisation; it has fed the body, healed the sick and refreshed the spirit. Of how many plants can we say as much?

Although water-lilies flourished in other countries from early times, their culture in this country is comparatively recent. The earliest reference in horticultural literature appears to be in Phillip Miller's *Gardener's Dictionary* (1731), where he says: 'In some gardens I have seen plants cultivated in large troughs of water, where they flourish very well and annually produce great quantities of flowers'. For about 100 years we hear little more of them until in 1839 Lindley drew up a description of the great *Victoria amazonica*—a water-lily-like plant—which had just flowered for the first time in England.

This remarkable plant attracted considerable attention, and people began to wonder if there were not other strange or beautiful plants which might be induced to bloom in this country. Consequently a craze for growing unusual aquatics swept the horticultural public and those with the money to construct a greenhouse built themselves a pool, and travellers sent home seeds and roots from all over the world. In 1851 a hybrid between *N. lotus* and the Indian *N. rubra* appeared in the tanks at Chatsworth, the home of the Duke of Devonshire. Named *devoniensis*, the large red flowers opened in the evening and were so handsome that they gave further impetus to a craze which persisted for many years.

In the hardy field, however, there was less material; *N. alba*, the British white, and *N. candida* and the rose *alba rubra* from Scandinavia, were known, later reinforced by

N. tuberosa and *N. odorata* from North America. Most of these were, however, white, and interest was lukewarm until at the close of the century came Marliac's colourful hybrids. No man has done more for the hardy water-lily than Latour Marliac—he brought the genus from semi-obscurity to an important and valued position in the water garden and his name will be for ever associated with the 'Queen of Aquatics'.

VARIETIES OF WATER-LILIES ARRANGED ACCORDING TO SIZE

Extra strong varieties for lakes and large ponds. Surface area, 6 to 10sq ft. Depth of water, $2\frac{1}{2}$ to 3ft.

WHITE

alba, our native species with a wide European distribution. Flowers 3 to 4in, foliage green; not as free as some of the hybrids.

'Albatross' (Marliac), attractive, glistening blooms, green leaves which are purple when young.

'Gladstoniana', of American origin, raised by Richardson of Lordstown, Ohio. The finest white, very large with golden stamens; foliage green.

'Gonnère' (Marliac), double flowers; not as free as the singles; foliage green.

'Marliacea Albida', pure white, sepals flushed pink, fragrant; large green leaves, red beneath.

tuberosa, a very strong grower from North America. Scented flowers June to September. There is a variety *maxima* with larger blooms and variety *Richardsonii* which is freer but not quite so robust.

PINK AND RED

alba rubra, a rare species only found in one protected lake in Sweden. It is uncommon in this country, but important as the parent of many of our pink forms. Flowers open pale pink, changing with age to deep red.

'Amabilis' (Marliac), star-shaped flowers, salmon-rose, deepening with age.

'Attraction' (Marliac), single garnet-red flowers, often 7 to 8in across.

'Colossea' (Marliac), flowers and leaves very large; will do in water up to 6ft; sweet-scented, petals flesh.

'Escarboucle' (Marliac), rich crimson. A very popular and beautiful variety with star-shaped flowers 8in across; extremely free.

'Goliath' (Marliac), tulip-shaped flowers with long petals; pinkish with orange-red petaloids.

'Leviathan' (Marliac), soft pink, free flowering.

'Lusitania' (Marliac), deep rose with mahogany stamens; foliage green, purple when young.

'Marguerite Laplace' (Marliac), fat pink blooms of good texture; very free and in bloom all the summer.

'Marliacea carnea' and 'Marliacea rosea' differ little except that the former is flesh-pink and the latter deep rose. Both are very free, fragrant, and make excellent cut blooms.

'Picciola' (Marliac), a very strong grower with large flowers, frequently 9 to 10in across, vivid amaranth-crimson. Extremely free.

'Souvenir de Jules Jacquier' (Marliac), also very vigorous, globular flowers of a mauvy-pink colour.

tuberosa rosea, sweet-scented form of the North American species with soft pink flowers; inclined to be rampant.

YELLOWS, ORANGES AND COPPERS

'Colonel Welch' (Marliac), the most prolific of all the yellow forms, with soft yellow blooms.

STRONG GROWING WATER-LILIES FOR MEDIUM-SIZED POOLS
Surface area, 5 to 7sq ft. Depth of water, 18 to 24in.

WHITE
'Gloire de Temple sur Lot' (Marliac), double creamy white.

'Loose', an American variety with flowers standing above the water; scented.

odorata, a North American species, sweet-scented, rhizomatous rootstock; foliage green.

'Virginalis', a beautiful Marliac hybrid, snow-white and in bloom all the summer.

The varieties 'Gonnêre' and 'Marliacea', already described, are also suitable for the medium-sized pool.

PINK AND RED
'Arethusa', of American origin, deep red.

'Atropurpurea', very unusual shade of dark crimson; young foliage crimson.

Brakeleyi Rosea, beautiful, fragrant, clear rose flowers standing just above water-level; very free, foliage green.

'Conqueror' (Marliac), red, flecked white, very free; young leaves purple.

'Darwin' (Marliac), red, striped white, scented; green foliage.

'Fabiola' (Marliac), rich pink with mahogany stamens; long season.

'Formosa' (Marliac), young flowers soft rose, deepening to red with age; golden stamens and green foliage.

'Galatée' (Marliac), rose, flecked and spotted white; foliage green mottled with purple.

'Gloriosa' (Marliac), large red flowers, very fine; long season.

'James Brydon', well-known North American variety with carmine-red, very squat flowers; free flowering and very adaptable.

'James Hudson' (Marliac), rich red-purple, petals narrow and star-like; very attractive.

'Mme Wilfron Gonnêre' (Marliac), fat, large, clear rose flowers.

'Marliacea rubra-punctata' (Marliac), rosy-carmine, spotted white.

'Masaniello' (Marliac), sweet-scented, globular, deep rose flowers; very free variety with long season.

'Murillo' (Marliac), bright rose, stellate flowers.

'Neptune', deep rosy-crimson, star-shaped flowers; young foliage purple.

'Newton' (Marliac), flowers standing out of the water, rose-vermilion, with orange stamens.

odorata, 'Helen Fowler', deep rose flowers standing above water level, sometimes 9in across; heavily scented.

odorata 'Turicensis', soft rose.

'René Gerard' (Marliac), rose, flecked crimson; very free.

'Rose Arey' Stellate, flowers of a rich rose shade, fragrant, and very free.

'Rose Nymphe', I consider this to be the finest pink water-lily, large open flowers 6 to 7in across, deep rose, very fragrant.

'Wm Doogue', flowers open shell-pink and fade to white with age.

'Wm Falconer', very deep red with yellow stamens; foliage purplish-red when young.

YELLOWS, ORANGES AND COPPERS

'Indiana' (Marliac), flowers opening orange-red, gradually changing to a brilliant shade of rich copper-red; foliage heavily spotted purple.

'J. C. N. Forestier' (Marliac), soft copper-rose, with flowers just above the water level.

'Lucida' (Marliac), rosy vermilion blooms with a darker centre; leaves blotched with purple.

'Marliacea Chromatella' and 'Moorei' are very similar with soft yellow flowers, very free and purple and brown variegated foliage.

'Sunrise', the best yellow water-lily with fragrant, rich golden flowers.

MEDIUM-GROWING WATER-LILIES FOR SMALL POOLS, TUBS, AND ROCK POOLS

Surface area covered: roughly 3sq ft. Depth of water: 12 to 18in. *denotes miniature kinds for 10in of water, covering an area 18 to 24in.

WHITE

'Albatross', very large golden anthers.

candida, species from Scandinavia and Asia which will grow in very cold water. There are many forms.

caroliniana 'Nivea', larger than preceding with fragrant, white flowers.

*odorata 'Minor', from North America; has tiny fragrant blooms and soft green leaves.

*pygmaea alba and tetragona, both miniature white-flowered forms for very small pools. Only botanical differences separate the two, which seed readily.

PINK AND RED

caroliniana, delicate rose-pink flowers which are very fragrant. It comes from North America. N. caroliniana rosea is an improved form.

'Ellisiana' (Marliac), the darkest of the small forms, with garnet red flowers.

'Eugenia de Land' (Marliac), medium-sized, stellate flowers of a rich pink colour standing just above the water.

'Fire Crest', deep pink with red-tipped stamens; fragrant.

'Froebeli' (Marliac), reliable free-flowering form with blood red blooms; one of the most popular.

'Laydekeri', a popular section of easily grown, free-flowering and medium-sized water-lilies, 'Fulgens' is crimson, 'Lilacea' soft rose, and 'Purpurata' crimson-spotted white.

'Marliacea Flammea', flowers amaranth flecked white; mottled foliage.

'Marliacea Ignea', vivid carmine blooms with glowing red anthers which are often petaloid.

odorata 'Exquisite' and *odorata* 'Luciana' are both good tub forms with rosy flowers; *odorata* 'Wm Shaw' is soft pink with a deep red zoning inside the blooms.

'Pink Opal', coral-pink flowers, good for cutting, and standing just above the water level.

*pygmaea 'Johann Pring', a new pygmy raised by Mr George Pring of the Missouri Botanic Garden. Flowers deep pink with orange stamens and frequently $2\frac{1}{2}$ in across.

'Suavissima', rosy-pink; fragrant.

YELLOWS, ORANGES AND COPPERS

'Andreana', dark red flowers overlaid with yellow. A variety that has fallen from fashion.

'Aurora', the flowers open yellow, are orange the second day and turn dark red on the third; very free with mottled foliage.

*'Chrysantha', blooms reddish-yellow, passing with age to cinnabar-red.

'Comanche', flowers rose overlaid apricot, deepening to copper-red, orange stamens.

'Graziella', reddish-yellow, becoming lighter with age; foliage variegated with purple.

odorata 'Sulphurea', sulphur-yellow flowers; variety 'Grandiflora' is an improved form.

'Paul Hariot', flowers open apricot-yellow and change with age to orange-pink and later deepen to red.

'Phoebus', yellow overlaid red with orange stamens.

pygmaea 'Helvola', soft yellow flowers about the size of a 5p-piece (shilling); foliage mottled. The plant is very free and is sometimes grown in a large bowl in a living-room.

'Robinsonian', yellow overlaid vermilion; foliage spotted.

'Seignoretti', orange-red petals with buff reverse.

'Sioux' (Marliac), flowers yellow suffused red, deepening to copper.

'Solfatare' (Marliac), flowers stellate, yellow flushed rose; foliage mottled.

CHAPTER VI

Other Choice Aquatics

WHILST water-lilies provide the chief ornament of the pool, the water garden will become more interesting if there are other kinds of plants as well. Different characteristics will recommend these aquatics; some may make smaller growth, others have curious or delicate leaves, and a few taller subjects will help to relieve the flatness of the formal pool. Unfortunately only a limited number of choice aquatics are hardy enough to winter outdoors in this country, and none of them can seriously vie with the water-lily for adaptability, charm, and colour range.

Nevertheless they have their uses—both from the aesthetic side and for the useful function of providing shade and cover for the animal occupants of the pond. It must be admitted that all are not of compact growth; there are some aquatics, in fact, which should be treated as pariahs, and never introduced to the water garden at all. Duckweed, *Potamogeton natans,* some typhas, and most sagittarias come into this category; they have the common fault of spreading too rapidly and vigorously. Unless completely emptied, the pond which once knows them knows them for ever; they resemble couchgrass and bindweed in the garden.

I would give, too, a word of caution when planting the edge of the pond. Don't use too much of the same subject! A clump of the compact, blue-flowered Pickerel Weed, or a few roots of Water Iris—with narrow, sword-like foliage—give you charm of the first order; don't cheapen the effect by too frequent use and repetition. It is far better to have one or two bold plantings of iris so that the leaves contrast with the other coarse lush foliage, than the piecemeal effect of odd roots dotted copiously all along the shore.

In the swampy ground that margins the pond you can have as many plants as you please—according to the width; such situations ought not to be wasted. The glory of the bog and water garden is at its height in late summer and early autumn, so plant for maximum pageantry at that time. As in the herbaceous border remember that it is mass plantings which give striking effects; bold splashes of colour draw attention to a plant in a way no amount of interplanting can. But vary the note, use a clump of a favourite plant in a big way and then have done with it; don't spoil the 'coup' by constant repetitions.

When it comes to compost these aquatics are not fussy. Heavy loam almost inclined to clay suits them well, although a few difficult plants, which seem to favour acid conditions, may be helped by the addition of a little peat. Crushed charcoal as a sweetening agent has some effects in sour soil and may be freely intermixed with loam.

The bulk of such aquatics is best planted in spring, although a certain amount of latitude may be allowed those with fibrous roots. It is policy to remove the old flower heads after blooming owing to the ideal conditions for germination, and when frost sears the leaves, cut top growth down to the water level. Dead vegetation at the waterside forms the snuggest of winter quarters for many pests, including the noxious water-lily beetle.

In this chapter are included only those aquatics which the author can personally recommend for decorative effects; secondary varieties have had to be omitted from this volume, but full descriptions and more about the plants are included in the more comprehensive *Water Gardening*.

Acorus

A. calamus var *variegatus*, is a variegated form of the common Sweet Flag, a well-known denizen of the Norfolk Fens. Like the type, all parts of the plant are aromatic and emit a warm, pungent odour when bruised or crushed. Growing 2 to 3ft high, the broad, strap-shaped leaves are green and white striped, and not unlike an iris in appearance. The flower is not spectacular, being a conical spadix 2 to 3in long of a greenish-brown colour. The plant is worth growing for its neat habit and variegated foliage; it should be planted with the rhizome just below the soil and in shallow water. Propagated by division.

Acorus calamus, the Sweet Flag, a well-known denizen of the Norfolk fens

A. gramineus is a Japanese species of slender growth, the foliage being narrow and rush-like and rarely more than 8 to 10in high. The neat tufted habit gives it some merit as a marginal aquatic, but the type is best passed over in favour of the variety *variegatus*. This is more conspicuous by reason of the yellow stripes on the leaves.

A. gramineus var *pusillus* is so distinct from the type plant that it probably merits specific rank. It does not flower in this country, but produces most attractive iris-like leaves and rhizomes a few inches in height. The dwarf habit limits its usefulness, but it is quaintly pretty in the rock-garden pool or may be used as a submerged subject in the cold-water aquarium. Of Japanese origin; propagated by division.

Anemopsis californica (syn *Houttuynia californica*)

An uncommon Californian aquatic which has proved hardy in this country. The rootstock is very aromatic and has some medicinal virtue, so that it is sold regularly in the drug markets of Mexico. Strung on necklaces—in the form of beads—it is sold as a specific against malaria, under the name of Yerba Mansa or Apache Beads. The general habit is reminiscent of the Japanese Anemones, the leaves being long-stalked, rounded at the base and mostly radical. The inflorescence consists of a conical spadix surrounded by a whorl of white petal-like bracts which give it the appearance of a flower of an anemone. The plant likes to grow in swampy places or shallow water which is not acid by nature. Propagated by division.

Aponogeton distachyos

The beautiful Water Hawthorn comes from a large family of decorative aquatics, most of which unfortunately are not hardy in this country. Its adaptability—since it is equally at home in 6in or 2ft of water—free-flowering habit and sweet scent make it a favourite subject with pond-owners, who find that best results come from spring planting and a heavy loam compost. The rootstock is small and conical, something like a large horse-chestnut, but bluish-black. The oblong leaves, borne straight from the base on long stems, float gracefully on the surface as do the forked spikes of black-and-white flowers. A strong vanilla fragrance from the latter explains the English name; they are borne freely throughout the summer months, with occasional stray blooms even during the winter. In rare instances, and in very sheltered localities, the plant may become a nuisance through persistent seeding. Should this occur it may be necessary to confine the roots in some form of container and regularly remove the old flower heads by means of a knife attached to a stick and a net. Pink- and rose-flowered varie-

Aponogeton distachyos, the sweet-scented water Hawthorn

ties have been known, and the flower heads are eaten in South Africa, its native habitat. Propagation by seed or division of the tubers.

A. krauseanum is another South African species which has proved hardy in shallow water in sheltered positions. Four to nine inches of water over the crown is ample during the growing period, but it may be necessary to protect the plant during very severe weather. This can be carried out in the manner suggested for water-lilies on page 28. The strap-shaped foliage is similar to, but paler in colour than that of *A. distachyos*, but the twin flower spikes are daintier and stand well out of the water. They are a uniform shade of creamy sulphur, sweetly scented, and seed freely. Other aponogetons have pink, white or blue flowers in single or twin flower spikes; unfortunately none of them is hardy.

Azolla caroliniana and A. filiculoides

A certain amount of floating vegetation is of the utmost value in a pool, since it provides shelter and shade for the fish and, by excluding the light, acts as a deterrent to the rapid multiplication of algae. It can be provided by floating leaves (as of water-lilies) or by a group of plants which can dispense with root anchorage and are borne on the surface and take their sustenance from the mineral salts dissolved in the water. There are but limited numbers of these and only a small proportion are hardy. The azollas, or Fairy Mosses, are not spectacular, but they are small and daintily branched, and of a pleasing green colour which changes to a rust-red in autumn. They increase rapidly in warm weather, but die down completely in the winter—to renew life from spores the following spring. In an exceptionally cold winter they may be killed altogether. *A. caroliniana* comes from the United States and tropical America, and *A. filiculoides*, which is the larger of the two, from the Andes and the west side of South America.

Brasenia schreberi (syn *B. peltata; Hydropeltis purpurea*)

An interesting aquatic which is widely distributed in all continents but Europe, but one which is not easy to grow. It seems to need water with an acid reaction and does not take kindly to the hard water of the London area. In brackish pools it will grow in a depth of 1 to 4ft, and it has small, rounded, floating leaves with the under-surfaces thickly coated with transparent jelly. The small purple flowers are borne in the axils of the leaves. Propagated by division of the roots or from seed.

Butomus umbellatus

Known as the Flowering Rush or Water Gladiolus, this is one of the handsomest of our native aquatics. Growing 2 to 4ft high, it has tapering, sedge-like leaves and umbels of showy pink flowers. It must be kept under control and

The Flowering Rush,
Butomus umbellatus

flowers more freely in shallow water. The seeds and roots were once used medicinally, and the baked tubers are still eaten in northern Asia. Propagation by division.

Calla palustris

The Bog Arum is one of those scrambling, creeping, irrepressible subjects so useful for disguising the hard line where concrete pond edge meets the land. The small, heart-shaped leaves, smooth and glossy, rise direct from the snake-like rhizome and the white flowers, resembling miniature Arum lilies, are succeeded by clusters of scarlet berries. The rootstock has been employed in bread-making in northern Sweden. Propagated by division of the rootstocks. Eastern North America, Europe, North Asia.

The Bog Arum, *Calla palustris*

Caltha palustris, the double-flowered variety *plena*

Caltha

Nearly all the Marsh Marigolds are worth a place in the bog garden, for they are free-flowering, easy to control and present no cultural problems. The grower should, however, be watchful of *C. polypetala*, the tallest species (2 to 3ft) from the Balkans, for this increases by means of stolons and can become a nuisance in a year or two if the roots are not confined. The golden flowers are large, sometimes 3in in diameter, and the dark-green leaves frequently 10 to 12in across. *C. palustris*, our native form, has much to commend it early in the year, for it is one of the first aquatics to flower. Growing 9 to 15in high the growth is compact, the leaves almost round, whilst the flowers, borne on branched stems, resemble giant buttercups. It will grow in shallow water or wet soil at the pond margin. The varieties *plena* and *monstrosa* have the merit of double flowers.

There are also several white-flowered forms, as *C. palustris alba* and *C. leptosepala*, but neither are as decorative as the golden varieties.

Catabrosa aquatica (syn *Glyceria aquatica* var *variegata*, *G. spectabile*)

A favourite aquatic grass, but nevertheless one to watch because of its spreading propensities. The foliage is attractively striped in green, yellow and white, and during the spring and autumn it is also suffused with a rosy tinting. Height 18 to 24in, the grassy inflorescence growing slightly taller. Suitable for a depth of 2 to 6in of water. Propagation by division.

Cotula coronopifolia BRASS BUTTONS

An attractive little annual for shallow water conditions, producing small golden flowers which resemble daisies with the outer florets removed. The foliage is narrow and toothed, and when crushed gives off an aromatic lemon verbena odour. It soon becomes colonised under suitable shallow water conditions. Africa, Australia.

Cyperus alternifolius UMBRELLA GRASS

An old fashioned grassy plant from Madagascar with 'umbrella' heads of foliage and numerous flat, pale-brown spikelets of flowers. It grows 1 to 3ft high and was much used years ago as a cottage-window plant. Not being perfectly hardy, it is policy to grow the plant in a pot, standing this at the pond margin for the summer months and removing it indoors for the winter. There are several varieties, the most attractive being *Gracilis*, slender and compact, 18in high, and var 'Variegatus', beautifully striated in green and white. The latter is sometimes available in florist shops, among collections of house plants. Other species, such as

C. congestus (syn *C. paramattensis*) and *C. vegetus* (syn *C. eragrostis*) grow about 2ft high and are hardy in shallow water in sheltered positions.

Damasonium alisma (syn D. stellatum)

A rare British aquatic of only local occurrence. Having the general characteristics of alisma, the oblong leaves are floating or just above the water surface with the flowers growing in whorls. Individual florets are white, with a yellow spot at the base of each petal, and the fruit is composed of six-pointed carpels, arranged in the form of a star, a feature which presumably accounts for the common name of Starfruit. Propagated from seed.

Decodon verticillatus (syn Nesaea verticillata)

A shrubby pond-side perennial growing up to 2ft in height. The habit and general appearance of the leaves is reminiscent of a willow, but the flowers are distinctive, being purple and salvia-like and borne in clusters in the leaf-axils. Its chief charm comes in autumn when the leaves glow with a rich crimson fire. Propagation is easily effected by cuttings. Eastern North America.

Dracocephalum palustre

A gay little shallow-water aquatic which deserves to be better known. Growing 12 to 15in high, several branching spikes bear quantities of bright rose flowers resembling those of dead nettles. The foliage is narrowly lanceolate with toothed margins. The plant is not rampant and if cut down after flowering will produce a second crop of flowers later in the season. Propagation by division or soft cuttings.

Echinodorus ranunculoides

An alisma-like aquatic less rampant than most of its near

relations, although even so the owner of a very small pool is advised to remove the old flower heads. An uncommon British plant, it grows about 12in high with narrow tapering leaves on long stems and showy umbels of rosy-white flowers. Suitable for shallow-water planting, it is propagated by seed.

Houttuynia cordata

An attractive little plant in a quiet sort of way. Growing 18 to 20in high, the stems are red, the bluish-green leaves large and heart-shaped, and the flowers white. The creeping rootstock should be planted in shallow water or in the bog garden. Himalayas to China and Japan. Propagated by division.

Hydrocharis morsus-ranae

Our native Frogbit; a graceful floating plant for the aquarium or pool, with small 1½in kidney-shaped leaves of a bright green colour and small, white, three-petalled flowers. Certain snails, particularly *Limnaea stagnalis*, are apt to prey upon the foliage, and the long trailing roots are also liable to become infested with algae.

Hydrocleys commersonii (syn *Linmocharis humboldtii; L. commersonii*)

Water Poppy. One of the most beautiful of flowering aquatics but only hardy in favoured positions. For good results, use sifted loam and set the plant in a pan or basket under 6 to 9in of water. The leaves are oval, fleshy, rich green, and float on the surface, whilst the handsome yellow, three-petalled flowers stand just above water level. Each bloom only lasts a day, but during the season the plant is very prolific and flowers freely throughout the summer. Brazil. Propagated by cuttings.

Iris

The Yellow Flag (*Iris pseudacorus*) is well known as an aquatic subject with its stately sword-like foliage and bright yellow blooms. Kept in bounds, it is an admirable plant for all types of water gardens, although of inferior beauty to its variegated counterpart, var *variegata*, or the soft primrose var *bastardii*.

Less well known, but of superior decorative qualities, is *I. laevigata* and its forms. For long this species from Japan and eastern Siberia was confused in gardens with the moisture-loving *I. kaempferi* largely because of mixing of plants and seedlings at the exit ports. *I. laevigata* is, however, truly aquatic, and for best results should be grown in 2 to 3in of water. It flowers freely from May to July and is in my opinion the finest hardy aquatic, next to the water-lily, that we have. The type has rich caerulean blue flowers with a golden spot on each claw, strap-shaped foliage less rigid than that of *I. pseudacorus* and reaches about 2ft in height.

The varieties are well worth growing for variation in colour; they include var Alba white; var Atropurpurea rich violet; and var 'Variegata', blue flowers and white striped foliage.

Iris pseudacorus variegata, a well-known aquatic subject with stately foliage and bright yellow blooms

Juncus

Out of a large genus (comprising some 225 species) there are but few rushes which can fairly be recommended for the water garden. For the most part the family is weedy, coarse-growing and extremely rampant, and should be rigorously eschewed. The forms given here are less encroaching and have some individuality which renders them attractive.

J. effusus var *aurea-striatus* is a golden variegated form of the common rush used for mats and seating and grows about 2½ft high. The thick, dark-green, round stems are longitudinally striped with yellow.

J. effusus var *spiralis* is almost grotesque. The stems have a 'permanent wave' which causes them to grow in a spiral fashion like a corkscrew. Height, 18in.

Both these varieties may be increased by division, and have to be watched for the appearance of normal green stems which must be immediately removed.

Ludwigia repens (Jussieva repens)

A pretty little plant from tropical and North America, which is hardy in normal winters, but might need protection under really Arctic conditions. The habit is scrambling; the long branching stems creeping along the margins and floating in shallow water. The leaves are small, olive-green and shining, and large single, golden-yellow flowers arise from the axils to stand just above water level. Easily propagated by division or cuttings.

Menyanthes trifoliata

The Bog Bean has a wide distribution in northern temperate regions, but only occurs locally in Britain. It is useful in the water garden as marginal cover, because of the versatility with which it adapts itself to life; in the water inside the pool or in the mud surround beyond. The plant has a snake-like scrambling stem from which emanate roots, dark-green broad-bean-like leaves and clusters of delicately fringed flowers of a pinkish colour. Individually they look like stars cut out of a piece of Turkish towelling.

The species is important medicinally for the tonic values of the rhizomes, and it has been used as a substitute for beer. It is propagated by division in spring.

Miscanthus saccharifer var variegata

The variegated form of the Hardy Sugar Cane is a fine perennial grass with beautifully striped leaves and feathery inflorescence. It grows about 6ft tall and should be planted in a key position in full sun and a rich moist soil. Ornamental grasses of striking appearance always command attention, and this variety will give much pleasure if planted so that the full beauty of its development may be appreciated. Propagated by division in spring.

Myosotis palustris

The Water Forget-me-not, with its bright blue florets, always pleases and should be planted with a liberal hand in the shallows at the streamside or pond margin. It may be propagated from seed or by division or cuttings in spring.

Myriophyllum proserpinacoides

A bog species of a genus generally renowned for its submerged aquatics. M. proserpinacoides comes from Central America and should be tender, but as a matter of fact it winters outside nine years out of ten. As a precautionary measure, however, it is a simple matter to strike a few cuttings in a pan of loam about September and keep these in the greenhouse or shed until the following May. The foliage is most attractive, growing in long feathery trails which turn red at the tips in autumn. It is an ideal subject for planting in fountain basins so that the green growth drops over the sides, or it may be used for marginal work at the pond edge. The common name is Parrot's Feather, presumably referring to its appearance in autumn.

Nephrophyllidium crista-galli (syn *Menyanthes crista-galli*)
This plant is by no means common, but attractive enough to merit purchase when opportunity occurs. The inflorescence of white flowers is so arranged as to resemble a Cock's Comb, a fact which has probably led to the adoption of this as its common name. The leaves are rounded, wavy at the edges, and the plant grows 18 to 24in high. It may be grown under bog conditions or in very shallow water. North America, Japan. Propagation by division.

Nuphar
A genus of coarse-growing aquatics allied to, but inferior to, the hardy water-lilies. The thick leathery foliage floats on the surface, as does that of the nymphaeas. Its toughness and vigour, however, give the genus a strong constitution so that one may grow nuphars, or Pond Lilies, under conditions where one could not hope to succeed with water-lilies. Deep water, running water and shade are not suitable locations for water-lilies, but nuphars will do in such situations. although naturally they thrive and flower better under more congenial conditions.

Many species have beautiful submerged foliage—crisped, translucent or membraneous; a feature which is specially noticeable in deep water. Aquarists with large tanks frequently use them for decorative effects in their aquaria.

The rhizomes grow horizontally, rather like the tuberous forms of water-lilies, and should be planted in heavy loam by the methods advocated for those plants. They should be introduced with caution to the small pool, for their irrepressible habits have a rather smothering effect on other plants and can become a nuisance. The flowers are smaller than those of the water-lilies, mostly yellow or orange, and have a strong vinous odour. Under suitable conditions they seed readily.

One of the best for the water garden is the Common Spatterdock, *N. advena*. This has tough oblong leaves, about a foot in length, standing well out of the water, and globular greenish- or purplish-yellow flowers 2 to 3in across. There is a variegated form.

N. japonicum var *rubrotinctum* is superior to its Japanese parent (*japonicum*) by reason of the fact that the flowers are orange-scarlet and have red-tipped stamens.

N. luteum is the British species and only suited to the wild garden; in more ornamental waters it should be passed over in favour of one of the other kinds mentioned.

N. pumilum, with pale yellow blossoms, is the baby of the family; free-flowering and eminently suited to rock pools with cold, still or flowing water. European.

N. polysepala from North America is a robust species with yellow flowers, frequently 4 to 5in across when grown in shallow water, and *N. rubrodiscum* is renowned for its beautiful membraneous foliage and the prominent red disc which occurs on the inner surface of the flowers.

The rootstocks of nuphar contain tannic acid and have been used in tanning, and there is also a fair amount of starch which has been extracted and used for bread making in Sweden. The Greeks prepare a cordial from the flowers and the leaves may be employed as a styptic.

Nymphoides nymphaeoides (N. peltata; Limnanthemum nymphaeoides)
Native member of a genus which gives us some beautiful

Nymphoides nymphaeoides, a hardy, yellow aquatic with floating flowers and leaves

aquatics. Unfortunately most of these are tender and a pool or pan of water in a greenhouse is necessary to grow them. The species indicated is hardy in 6 to 18in of water and grows after the manner of a water-lily, with floating leaves, rounded and wavy at the margins, light green, mottled with maroon and chocolate. The flowers are yellow, fringed at the edges, and stand several inches above the water. The plant has some tonic properties and has been used in medicine. There is a form *bennettii* with plain green leaves.

Orontium aquaticum

An interesting perennial of the Arum family with yellow finger-like blooms. It is adaptable, growing in wet mud at the pondside with the same ease that it conditions itself to an existence in water from 2 to 18in deep.

In the former situation the foliage is profuse and sturdy, with large leaves of a glaucous blue shade occasioned by a protective coating of wax. In deep water, however, they are more strap-shaped and float on the surface. Height, 12 to 18in. Propagation by division or seed.

In its native North America cattle, hogs and stags are reputed to eat the leaves, and the Indians use the seeds and roots for food. The English name of the plant is Golden Club; its roots penetrate deeply so that plenty of soil should be provided.

Peltandra

The Arrow Arums deserve wider cultivation, for they are easy to grow, do not encroach, and are quite decorative. *P. alba*, the white Arrow Arum, has broad, arrow-shaped leaves on 12 to 18in stems, and a white arum-like flower

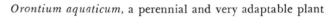

Orontium aquaticum, a perennial and very adaptable plant

which is succeeded by scarlet berries. The rhizome is fleshy and has been used for food.

P. virginica, the Green Arrow Arum, has green flowers followed by green berries and firm, narrowly arrow-shaped leaves. Both plants come from eastern North America and are propagated by division in spring. They should be planted in groups in shallow water.

Penthorum sedoides

Not a spectacular plant, but effective in the autumn when the foliage assumes such gay tints that it has been nicknamed Joseph's Coat. It is of shrubby habit with narrow, lanceolate foliage and greenish-white spikes of flowers. Height, 18in. North America. Propagated by cuttings or division.

Pontederia cordata

The North American Pickerel Weed is one of the first choices after the water-lilies for the outdoor garden pool. It is hardy, decorative, not a 'gate-crasher', and, moreover, has blue flowers, which are not so easily come by in aquatics. Normally growing 18 to 24in in height, it produces smooth, glossy spear-shaped leaves and crowded spikes of soft blue flowers. There is a taller growing variety (4 to 5ft) called *lancifolia*, but for some reason it is not quite so hardy. Roots should be planted in spring, under 3 to 5in of water, in a good rich loam and, when autumn frosts cut the stems, reduce these down to the water level. Propagated by division or seed.

Potentilla palustris (syn Comarum palustre)

A British plant which likes acid conditions and does not always thrive in our hard London water. It is sometimes known as Purple Marshlocks on account of the dingy purple

Pontederia cordata 'Lancifolia', a blue - flowered variety growing 4-5ft high

buttercup-like flowers. The leaves resemble strawberry foliage and the whole plant reaches some 12in in height. Propagated from the stolons which are just detached from the parent root and planted.

Ranunculus lingua 'Grandiflora'

An improved form of the Spearwort, a British native. It grows 2 to 3ft high, with narrow lanceolate leaves and branching stems of very large golden, buttercup-like flowers. It is in bloom during the late spring and summer and grows under marsh conditions or in an inch or two of water. Propagation is effected by division in spring.

Sagittaria sagittifolia plena (S. japonica)

This sterile double-flowered Arrowhead is the only variety I can recommend for planting in a small pool for

An improved form of the Spearwort, *Ranunculus lingua*
'Grandiflora'

most of the others seed or increase too rapidly for a confined situation. The spikes of large double-white flowers are very handsome and not unlike a double Brompton Stock. They grow about 15in high, and the foliage is smooth and deeply arrow-shaped.

Very deep water is not conducive to flowering, and the tubers are best set 1 to 1½in deep under loam, with 3 to 5in of water above that. Propagation is controlled by the number of tubers produced and is somewhat slow.

Saururus

The American Swamp Lily *S. cernuus*, is reputed to reach 5ft in its native clime, but rarely exceeds 2ft in Britain. It should be grown in wet soil or very shallow water, and has bright green heart-shaped leaves and 4 to 6in spikes of nodding, fragrant white flowers. Propagated by division in spring.

S. chinensis is the Lizard's Tail from China and has spikes of yellowish-white blossoms and oval leaves. Height, 12 to 16in. Propagated by division.

Scirpus tabernaemontani 'Zebrinus'

A true Bulrush with fat, round stems 4 to 5ft in height and alternately barred in green and white. It has a bizarre appearance when well grown, and for best effects should be colonised in shallow water. Any plain green stems which appear should be cut out to preserve the variegated feature which constitutes its chief charm. Propagation by division in spring.

There is another Bulrush called *laetivirens* var 'Aureus', which has the striping arranged vertically around the stems; the variegations, however, are more golden than white in this instance.

Senecio smithii

Curiously enough, there are comparatively few aquatic representatives of the largest plant order—*Compositae*—so that this plant is particularly welcome.

The original stock was discovered by Captain Cook in Cape Horn, but, in spite of the time it has been in this country, it is still not well known. Growing 2 to 3ft high, it has dark-green, tough, broadly oblong leaves and heavy heads densely covered with large white daisy-like flowers. Propagated by division in spring. It needs only very shallow water.

Thalia dealbata

A handsome foliage plant somewhat resembling a canna or hedychium. Growing 3 to 5ft high, the leaves are a greyish green and the flowers, borne on arching wands, are small and of a reddish-purple colour. The plant is dusted with a fine white powder which gives it a frosted appearance. Although it comes from North America it is doubtfully hardy, and stock plants should always be kept inside in reserve. Since the plant is somewhat scarce and expensive it is perhaps politic in any case to grow it in large flower-pots and submerge these in the pool for the summer months only. Propagation by division in spring, using a rich compost.

Trapa natans

The species is the best known of a genus of some eight aquatic annuals with large edible, chestnut-like fruits. The seed must be kept moist to preserve its vitality and is sown in shallow pans of loam and water. The plant is of branching habit with small holly-shaped leaves, upheld in the water so that they float by swollen, pinkish, 2 to 4in long petioles. These are filled with spongy parenchymatous tissue which makes them buoyant. The flowers are axillary, small and white, and later give place to the seeds, which are about the size of a chestnut, black and hard with four spinescent angles. They contain much farinaceous matter and are sold for food in southern Europe under the name of Water Chestnuts.

As the species is native to the warmer parts of Europe, Asia and Africa it sometimes fails outside in very severe winters. When well established in a sheltered pool however it may persist for years—especially if a warm summer ripens the seeds.

Typha

These two Reedmaces are the only kinds the cautious gardener will introduce to his pool, for most of the family increase from the running rootstocks at a frightening rate.

T. laxmannii (syn *stenophylla*) is a slender plant $2\frac{1}{2}$ to 4ft tall with very narrow leaves, easily stirred by the slightest breath of wind, and typical spikes of 'bulrush'-like flowers.

T. minima is more diminutive, growing only 12 to 18in high, but free-flowering and very dainty. Both kinds are increased by division and should be grown in concrete pockets or containers.

Villarsia

A genus of yellow-flowered, chiefly Australian water plants suitable for growing in the shallows. Propagation is readily effected by seed or division, and the plants are hardy enough except in exceptional winters when they should be protected.

V. ovata (syn *Menyanthes ovata*) grows 6 to 12in high and has oval foliage and racemes of citron-yellow, fringed petalled flowers.

V. parnassifolia is taller (1 to 2ft), with soft yellow blooms, and *V. reniformis* is characterised by more rounded leaves and heavy panicles of golden flowers. Height, 1 to 2ft.

Zantedeschia aethiopica (syn *Calla aethiopica*)

The common Arum Lily likes plenty of water during the growing season and is frequently used at the pond margin during the summer months. The glossy arrow-shaped leaves and large white flowers command admiration and look impressive when growing in clumps or bordering the stream. They reach 2 to 3ft in height, and the blooms are pleasantly fragrant.

The variety called 'Little Gem' is useful in the rock garden, for it is much smaller (12in), with a 3 to 4in flower spathe.

CHAPTER VII

Submerged Aquatics

NATURE shows such perfection of planning and foresight in the intricacies of life that it becomes true to say that nothing is in this world without a purpose. All life is provided with the means to breathe and feed and reproduce itself, and in the wonderful interdependencies of one form of existence with another we see a guiding hand which 'shapes our ends, rough hew them as we will'.

If we keep fish in our pool they have to feed and breathe and a munificent Providence provides them with the wherewithal in the most natural manner. Insects and microscopic water life provide the food, and plants supplement the diet. Air is absorbed at the water surface from the atmosphere and augmented by a supply of oxygen provided by the plants. The miracle of the green leaf has been extolled by botanists frequently in the past, but, since it touches so closely on the welfare of the water garden and to some may not be familiar, I may be forgiven for a moment's digression.

We are all aware that fish (and other livestock) in the pond take in oxygen and breathe out carbon dioxide—behave, in fact, in the same way as ourselves. Carbon dioxide in excess can be poisonous, and it is easy to realise that a crowded pond may become depleted of oxygen at a faster rate than it is being returned by absorption at the surface. In hot weather this is particularly noticeable, and many will be familiar with the sight of goldfish swimming at the surface under such conditions, and endeavouring to gain relief by gulping atmospheric air. When this happens the balance is not right and, alternatively, the number of fish must be reduced or the aeration improved—either artificially from a pump (which chills the water) or by adding more plants.

On the leaf surface and more particularly on the underside, there are numbers of small pores called *stomata*, each protected by a pair of kidney-shaped guard cells which have some control over the size of the aperture. They may be readily seen with the aid of a microscope and are so plentiful that, as Professor Salisbury tells us in his wonderful book, *The Living Garden*, there are over a million on the underside of an apple leaf.

One of their functions in land plants is to pass off water vapour, taken up by the roots and superfluous to the plant's requirements once the mineral salts dissolved in it have been extracted. But they are also a means of entrance and exit for various gases needed by the plant in its daily life. Green plants are the world's chemists and they alone have the power to manufacture food from the atmosphere, a miracle which is brought about by the combination of carbon dioxide, the green tissue of the plant (called chlorophyll), water and sunlight. The sun provides the energy, and the chlorophyll is enabled with its aid to extract the carbon dioxide and with the assistance of water taken up by the roots turn it into sugar. This is the simplest form of plant food, but for convenience in storage the plant often converts it into starch until needed, as in the tubers of sagittaria, butomus, etc.

The carbon, then, has been retained, but the oxygen is redundant and so is returned to the air or water via the stoma. And so we see that the plant has reversed the process of breathing as practised by animal life, each utilising the waste products of the other. At the risk of confusing the issue, however, I must say that plants do respire—ie they take in oxygen and discharge carbon dioxide—at all times of the day from all parts of the plant. Under the influence of light, however, this operation is almost completely masked by the more vigorous process of carbon assimilation, and the small amount of oxygen they breathe makes little difference to pool conditions.

Nature has so arranged things that there are some aquatic plants so active in performing this carbon assimilation that they have been termed oxygenators, and their services in maintaining the oxygen content of water in which fish are present is most important. Adopting an entirely aquatic existence, they are mostly completely submerged and quite insignificant in appearance.

It behoves the owner of a fish pond to introduce a number to his pool for, besides this useful function, they provide food for the fish, depositories for their eggs and shelter for the fry against the cannibalistic pursuits of their parents. For convenience in planting they are best set as slips in pans or boxes of loam and lowered into position in the pool; they may be introduced any time during the spring and summer.

In the pool, beauty of form with these plants will not matter since they will be little seen, but it *is* important to ensure that they are good oxygenators and not inclined to become rampant. In the aquarium the position is a little different. Besides their usefulness the plants will have an aesthetic value in forming a background to enhance the naturalness of the conditions under which the fish are kept.

Variety of plant, leaf-shapes and colouring are important in this instance, but hardly matter in the pool. For aquarium work there is a tendency to use bog plants as submerged aquatics; it must be remembered, however, that their oxygenating powers are less pronounced than those of the true underwater plants.

When gathering plants from wild sources, always thoroughly wash them before planting. There is a very real risk of introducing hydra and other pests in this way—not to mention algae in all their forms.

In the following list A. denotes suitability for the outdoor pool, B. for the cold-water aquarium, and C. for the tropical tank.

Anacharis (syn *Elodea*) WATER THYME A. B.

One of the best oxygenators with closely packed stems of small dark green leaves, bearing a faint resemblance to thyme. It needs to be watched in outdoor pools. *A. canadensis* is also known as the Canadian Pondweed. *A. callitrichoides*, more slender in habit than the preceding, is another useful plant. America. Propagated from slips.

Anubias lanceolata C.

A marsh aroid from French Guinea which will condition itself to a subdued light and underwater conditions in the tropical aquarium. The foliage is boat-shaped, rich green, 5 to 6in in length and the flowers resemble green arums with whitish tips. Propagated by division.

Apium inundatum B.

A poor oxygenator with attractive watercress-like leaves above the water and thread-like ones beneath. It is frequently found in streams and ditches. It needs renewing often if the light is not good.

Aponogeton crispus C.

A beautiful 'set-piece' plant for the tropical tank. Growing 6 to 12in high, the narrow, lance-like leaves are somewhat translucent and ripple attractively at the edges. The
flowers are white and borne on forked spikes just above
water level. Propagated from seed. Ceylon.

Aponogeton fenestralis (syn *Ouvirandra fenestralis*) C.

The Madagascar Lace Plant, a highly prized acquisition
for the tank, but scarce in supply and temperamental in
growth. It prefers a subdued light and does best in a
wooden receptacle. The forked creamy-white flowers thrust
above the water are reminiscent of *A. krauseanum*, but its
greatest attraction lies in the foliage which is dark green
and skeletonised. It is a poor oxygenator.

Aponogeton ulvaceus C.

This fine plant from Madagascar has delightful submerged foliage, crimped and waved at the edges like a
Hart's Tongue Fern. The leaves are latticed and semi-translucent, and white flowers rise just above water level. The
plant takes a resting period during the winter, but starts
up again in spring. Reproduction by division.

Cabomba B.

The Fanworts are good oxygenators, but soon become
leggy and constantly need to have the tops taken off and
replanted. The leaves are deeply segmented and dark green
in colour, and small yellow or white flowers appear just
above the surface. Best-known species is *C. caroliniana* and
its reddish-leaved variety *rosaefolia*.

Callitriche WATER STARWORT A. B.

Excellent oxygenators with pale green foliage which rises

to the surface and forms pale starry masses. Goldfish are very partial to it. It needs constant renewal in the aquaria as the dense top growth induces discoloration and thinness in the lower leaves. The stems are tangled and difficult to sort out, so the plants are best set in clumps. *C palustris* is most useful in spring and summer and *C. hermaphroditica* is more active during the autumn months. Both are British plants.

Cardamine lyrata B. C.

A fine Japanese erstwhile bog plant with delicate rounded leaves poised on very slender stems; dainty and fragile-looking, but nevertheless quite tough. A good oxygenator, it bears some resemblance to Moneywort (*Lysimachia nummularia*). Propagated by cuttings.

Ceratophyllum HORNWORT A.

Brittle-natured plants with bristle-like leaves arranged in whorls around the stems. They will grow in very cold and deep water, but are not satisfactory in the aquarium because easily damaged. *C. demersum* and *C. submersum* are both British species.

Chara STONEWORT A.

These bear some resemblance to the preceding, being brittle and with the foliage cut to a needle fineness. They are, moreover, rough to the touch and unpleasant to smell. The family should not be introduced into small pools, as they grow so rapidly. There are a number of British species of which the best known are *C. aspera*, *C. fragifera* and *C. fragilis*.

Cryptocoryne WATER TRUMPET C.

Arum-like plants from tropical America and the Malayan

Archipelago, which on account of their slow growth are much favoured by aquarists. Shallow water plants, they will adapt themselves to an aquarium existence and will persist almost longer than any plant I know in a subdued light. Propagated by runners or corms. The flowers are mostly reddish-purple, sweetly scented and standing above the water. Principal kinds grown are *C. beckettii*, very small (7in), narrow leaves of a delicate green; *C. ciliata*, 1ft long, thick, narrow-stalked leaves of a uniform green shade; *C. cordata*, leaves oblong on stout stems, 1ft, olive-green with greenish-purple undersurfaces, prominent veining; *C. griffithii*, broadly cordate foliage, dark green with a satiny sheen, flowers dark red, the most robust species; *C. willisii*, distinguished by the ripple-edged foliage, not very big.

Echinodorus intermedius AMAZON SWORD PLANT C.

A good centre-piece for the tropical aquarium with short-stemmed but large, bright green leaves, broadly strap-shaped. It may be left undisturbed a long time in the tank and is propagated by the runners which emanate from its crown. A good oxygenator, but overpowering in a very small tank. Height, 18 to 24in. Flowers rosy-white above water level. Brazil.

E. radicans, a robust plant and a good oxygenator. Broad, heart-shaped leaves of a pale green colour and semi-translucent. Flowers white. Central America. Propagated from seed.

Egeria densa B.

An excellent oxygenator for the cold aquarium, although it shows a tendency to rot off in warm water. Well known in the trade as *Elodea densa*, it is not unlike a giant anacharis, but merits specific rank because the white three-petalled

flowers are insect pollinated. True elodeas bear insignificant flowers which are fertilised under water. It comes from
the Argentine and is only hardy in very sheltered positions
in this country. Propagated by breaking off pieces and
planting.

Eleocharis acicularis HAIRGRASS A. B. C.

A dainty grass of tufted habit with hair-like stems 5 to
6in in height. It is really a bog plant, and when submerged
sometimes grows taller. Of a pleasing shade of green, it
multiplies by runners and forms a fine contrast with the
other aquarium plants. Britain.

Fontinalis antipyretica WILLOW MOSS A. B.

A British plant which is usually found growing in rivers
or streams attached to stones or pieces of wood. It is about
the darkest green in colour of any of the submerged aquatics and flows out in rich mossy patches. *F. gracilis* is smaller
and more thread-like; in the aquarium it soon becomes
covered with sediment. W. Innes, in his excellent book
Goldfish Varieties and Water Gardens, says that the American aquarist makes practical use of this faculty. As soon as
the plants are covered with sediment they are taken out,
rinsed and returned. As the stems are strong they stand this
treatment, and it is a useful means of clearing the water.
Both species are European and *F. antipyretica* is found in
Britain.

Heteranthera dubia WATER STAR GRASS C.

An uncommon little aquatic with bronzed grassy foliage
and small bright yellow flowers lying flat on the water surface. It is easy to grow, does not attract algae and merits
more general cultivation. Tropical America. Propagated by
division.

Hottonia palustris WATER VIOLET A. B.

A charming British water plant of local occurrence, with pretty pinnately divided foliage and whorls of lilac flowers standing 8 to 10in above water level. Winter buds are produced in the autumn, which sink to the bottom of the pond and reappear in the spring. The plant breaks away to the surface to flower in early summer.

Hydrilla verticillata C.

An elodea-like plant with stems densely clothed with dark-green, narrow leaves. They are, however, short and stiffer than those of that genus, but the plant is a good oxygenator. Propagated from cuttings. India and Ceylon.

Hydrotrida caroliniana (now more correctly *Bacopa amplexicaulis*)

A Central American aquatic with thick, oval leaves on a stout stem. The plant is slightly hairy throughout and has rich blue axillary flowers. These, however, only appear when the plant is grown in shallow water. A slow grower under aquarium conditions, it has a pungent smell.

Hygrophila polysperma C.

A handsome aquatic plant from India for the tropical tank. Bearing some resemblance to ludwigia, the leaves are arranged in opposite pairs and are bright green and tapered with purplish stems and veining. It runs along the bottom of the tank, rooting freely at the nodes, and is more probably a bog plant than a true submerged aquatic.

Isoetes lacustris QUILLWORT A.

A dwarf (4 to 6in) aquatic, from the bottom of northern lakes, with quill-like, rounded, dark green leaves. Fish feed on the foliage. Propagated from spores or by division.

Lagarosiphon major (syn *Elodea crispa*) A. B.

A first-class oxygenator long grown in this country under the name of *Elodea crispa*. It comes from South Africa, but is hardy in normal winters and may be recommended with every confidence for pools, lakes and cold water aquaria. The sturdy texture simplifies control, and this fact, coupled with its most efficient oxygenating powers, renders the plant one of our best submerged aquatics. In general habit it resembles a giant elodea, with many narrow leaves clasping the stem, each reflexed inwards so as to give the plant a 'curly' appearance. Propagated from slips.

Limnophila heterophylla (syn *Ambulia heterophylla*) C.

This species and that of *L. sessiliflora* constitute good oxygenators for warm-water tanks. Somewhat resembling Cabomba, the plants, when well grown, are a vivid shade of almost emerald green. Both species come from tropical Asia and need a good compost if they are to do well. Some of the finest plants I ever saw were in the tanks of Dutch aquarists—in a medium of clay, loam, sand and peat. Propagated by cuttings.

Littorella uniflora (syn *lacustris*) SHORE GRASS A. B.

A British marginal plant sometimes used for submerged work. In general appearance it somewhat resembles Isoetes, with rounded green leaves, 2 to 4in in height, but the flower more nearly resembles that of a Plantain. Propagated by division.

Lobelia dortmanna WATER LOBELIA A.

Anyone who has seen this plant growing really well will never forget it, for the spikes of soft blue flowers, when borne in masses, standing 9 to 12in above water level, are both impressive and beautiful. I have seen it in Sweden growing just so, but it is also a British plant. The foliage comes in tufts 1 to 2in high, and the plant throws up long stems to flower. It usually grows at the margins of deep, clear lakes with a sandy bottom, and is not easy to transplant unless conditions are identical with the habitat.

Ludwigia A. B. C.

L. palustris and *L. natans* are further examples of bog plants utilised for decorative effects as submerged aquatics. They are good-tempered and live under such conditions for considerable periods, but have no oxygenating value. The stout, reddish stems are plentifully clothed with stout, oval shining leaves and are olive-green with a reddish reverse. Their leathery texture precludes the growth of much algae so that they keep remarkably clean. Propagated by division or cuttings, *L. natans* comes from South America, but *L. palustris* is localised in Britain.

Lysimachia nummularia B.

The common Creeping Jenny and its variety *aurea*, with golden foliage, are such adaptable plants that they grow almost anywhere. The aquarist uses them at times in his cold-water tanks. Propagated by cuttings or division.

Myriophyllum WATER MILFOIL A. B. C.

The genus is a large one, embracing species from all over the world, uniform in possessing finely cut, feathery whorls of foliage. The inflorescence is in all cases insignificant, but the plants are good oxygenators, although subject to attention from confervae and algae.

The British forms, *M. spicatum, verticillatum* and *alterniflorum*, are suitable for the outdoor pond; and *heterophyllum, pinnatum* and the reddish forms known as *rubrifolium* for indoor work. Increased by cuttings.

Najus flexilis A.

A true underwater plant, but not desirable for pool planting because of the brittleness which renders it continuously untidy. It is an annual, but seeds freely from the inconspicuous axillary flowers. Whorls of light green leaves, narrow and curled, are borne at intervals on a branching stem. Propagated by slips. Europe, including the British Isles.

Nasturtium officinale (more correctly *Rorippa nasturtium-aquaticum*) WATER CRESS

This common salading makes for variation of foliage in the cold-water aquarium. Small slips about 6in long are set into the compost; they need frequent renewal.

Nitella gracilis A. B.

The commonest species of a group of chara-like plants, all good oxygenators. Foliage and stems are narrow and of an olive-green shade, but grow so thickly that they make excellent cover for young fry. Inclined to spread under certain conditions of warmth and shallow water. England. Propagated by slips.

Potamogeton PONDWEEDS B.

An extensive genus of mostly underwater plants, although some species—such as *P. natans*—have floating leaves. The majority are so weedy that I hesitate to recommend them for the outdoor pool, particularly *P. natans*, which will usurp a whole tank in the space of a year or two. A number of pondweeds grow in this country, nearly all in running water. *P. densus*, with wavy-edged, almost translucent, 3 to 4in leaves, is the most adaptable for aquarium work, but is not long-lived in confined quarters.

Proserpinaca palustris MERMAID WEED A. B.

An uncommon but worthy oxygenating plant from North America with two types of foliage—the submerged finely cut into needle segments and the floating leaves nettle-like with serrated edges. Small greenish-white flowers are borne just above water level. Propagated by cuttings.

Ranunculus aquatilis WATER CROWFOOT A. B.

A well-known British plant easily recognised by the small, white, buttercup-like flowers starring the water in early spring. Submerged foliage is finely cut, but the floating leaves are three-lobed and rounded. Propagated by slips. A short-lived plant in the aquarium, but suitable for still or running water out of doors. *R. delphinifolius* from North America also has two types of foliage, but in this case the flowers are yellow.

Sagittaria ARROWHEAD A. B. C.

The genus gives some of the most effective oxygenators, especially for aquarium work; the roots being spreading and penetrative keep the compost in healthy condition and fully utilise the waste products from the fish. The under-water foliage is the only type desired, and when aerial leaves appear they may be removed. The submerged foliage is oblong and grass-like, varying in width and vigour with the variety. Any of the following may be recommended with confidence: *S. cristata, graminea, natans* and *subulata*. Propagated from the runners.

Tillaea recurva A. B. (more correctly *Crassula recurva*)

An Australian marsh plant of creeping habit which readily adapts itself to a submerged existence in pond and cold-water aquarium. It has minute green foliage and tiny white flowers. Propagated by division.

Utricularia BLADDERWORT A. B. C.

A large genus of curious plants characterised by the presence of entire or rudimentary bladders, adapted in some cases for the capture of small insect life. The aquatic forms generally grown, such as *U. prehensilis, vulgaris* and *intermedia*, float in tangled patches in the water and trap small creatures, such as daphnia and cyclops, in the small bladders attached to the stems. The British *U. vulgaris* bears spikes of yellow snapdragon-like flowers above water level. Propagated by division.

Vallisneria TAPE GRASS B. C.

Very important aquarium plants with ribbon-like, grassy leaves, of good oxygenating ability. Male and female flowers are borne on separate plants; the former (containing the pollen) appearing as white sacs at ground level just above the roots, whilst the female flowers are carried on long spiral stalks which gracefully unwind to bring the stigma to water-surface level. When ripe the male sac bursts, the pollen grains rise to the surface, and when a female flower is pollinated the spiral stalk retracts, bringing the bloom below the surface to mature its fruit. In this country, however, fertile seed is not produced. Propagated by runners. The usual species for aquarium work is *V. spiralis*, but there are varieties with twisted leaves, such as var *torta*; and giant forms, var *gigantea* (up to 6ft in length and 1½ to 2in wide) and *gigantea rubrifolia*, with reddish leaves.

Zannichellia palustris HORNED PONDWEED A.

A weedy plant with tangled masses of thread like stems and tiny leaves. Europe, including Britain. Propagated by division.

CHAPTER VIII

A Few Good Tender Aquatics

MOST of the water plants referred to in this work have been
of a hardy nature, just as the details of pond construction
have applied to the garden rather than the greenhouse. It
is true that mention was made in the last chapter of tender
underwater objects—chiefly because aquaria are more generally owned than decorative glasshouses. Nevertheless, the
basic principles of tank construction and aquatic culture
are the same inside and out and, for the benefit of those
few possessing indoor pools, a brief list is given of tender
water plants which might be grown in such situations.
Provided frost is excluded, much heat during the winter
months is not essential, but warmth is required about Feb-
ruary or March (60° to 65° F), in which the plants must be
kept going until all danger of frost is over and the sun's
warmth increases in power.

THE TENDER WATER-LILIES

Methods of cultivation for the tender water-lilies differ
materially from that of their hardy relatives, just as the
blooms are distinct and the plants freer flowering and more
prodigal with seed. When obtained from the nurseryman

the tuber—resembling a black, elongated horse-chestnut seed—will be already started and carry several pairs of leaves. It will probably arrive about the end of May or June, and should be planted straight away in a rich compost of loam and rotted manure. Once it becomes established growth will be very rapid.

The tender water-lilies require plenty of room, otherwise the quality and quantity of bloom suffer. The flowers are borne 8 to 12in above water level and are usually sweetly scented; they make good cut flowers. There are kinds which open in the evening, remain full all night and close about 10 am next day, and others which open out in the morning, are in character all day and fold up towards evening. The colour of the bloom varies: there are white, pink, deep-red, purple, all shades of blue and even yellow forms, the art of the hybridist having supplemented a wide natural colouration range.

Chief difficulty experienced by growers has hitherto been the art of wintering the tubers: many indeed treating them as annuals. This has largely been due to a tendency to keep the larger tubers, which frequently rot away, rather than the small pea-sized 'spawn' found around the parent stock. When the plants die down in autumn the roots should be lifted, cleaned and the old tuber discarded. The youngsters may be stored in clean, slightly moist sand in a frostproof place. It is necessary to protect them against mice, which are partial to anything of a starchy nature during the winter months. In spring the young tuber is set in a 60 flower-pot in pure sand, *two inches* below the surface. This is stood in a bowl of water in a temperature round about 65° or 70° F. In a short time floating leaves will appear and when this happens, run the fingers down to beneath this growth and pinch off the shoot just above the tuber. The young plant may then be potted in a loam-and-sand mixture and grown on in the usual way. Meantime the tuber in the flower-pot will produce another crown which may be removed in similar fashion. Sometimes three or four plants may be obtained from one tuber in this way.

According to Mr Innes, the American grower, tubers from day-blooming varieties dependably carry on the characteristics of their parents, but those from night-blooming hybrids are less dependable and may show variations in colour. Small tubers may be kept dry for twelve months and retain their vitality, but in slightly moist, clean sand they will retain the 'germ of life' several years. As already stated, most tender water-lilies set seed freely. The swelling pods remain below the surface until ready to dehisce, when they rise and send forth quantities of seeds which float on the surface for about twenty minutes. If seed is required it is thus necessary to catch them immediately on release. This can be ensured by the precaution of fastening a muslin bag round the pod and securing this to a stake. The seed should be sown at once in shallow pans of sifted loam, barely covered with water, in a temperature of 65° to 70° F.

Some of the species of tender water-lilies are very interesting, especially *Nymphaea caerulea*, cited by many authorities as the Blue Lotus of the Nile. It bears sky-blue flowers 6 to 7in across with black-spotted sepals. Nowadays, however, the species are often passed over in favour of the fine hybrids raised by American hybridists, notably Mr Pring at the Missouri Botanic Gardens at St Louis. The following varieties are representative and have been grown in this country.

DAY-BLOOMING

August Koch, rich violet blue with unusual shadings, very free, fragrant. Produces young plantlets in viviparous fashion on the leaves.

General Pershing, a popular variety with flowers sometimes 8 to 10in across, very free and delightfully fragrant.

Henry Shaw, campanula-blue, flat flower, yellow stamens, very large and extremely free.

Mrs C. W. Ward, star-shaped pink flowers freely produced.

Mrs Edward Whitaker, very large lily with thin lavender-blue, very numerous petals.

Mrs Geo. Pring, the best of the white kinds with stellate, fragrant flowers of good size.

Panama Pacific, another viviparous kind with curious plum-purple or wine-shaded flowers with yellow stamens tipped with purple. The buds are heavily spotted bronze. This has proved one of the hardiest and freest forms for general cultivation in Britain.

Peach Blow, a Pring seedling with very solid flowers, outer petals rich pink, tending towards peach and even apricot towards the centre of the flower.

Rio Rita, another Pring hybrid of a rich pinkiness which nearly reaches red; very good.

St Louis, the first yellow tropical water-lily hybrid raised by Mr Pring and the first water-lily to be patented in America. Flowers 8 to 10in across when well grown; rich gold shade.

William Stone, rich blue, very free flowering, star-shaped, 8in across.

NIGHT-BLOOMING TROPICAL LILIES

Bissetii, cup-shaped, glowing rose, 8 to 10in across, with reddish-brown stamens, double flowers. Dark leaves with wavy edges.

Emily Grant Hutchings, cup-shaped, amaranth-red flowers of very large size and substance; foliage bronzed. Frequently stays open until mid morning.

Frank Trelease, glowing dark crimson, 8 to 10in, across, with reddish-brown stamens; long grown in this country.

George Huster, red velvety crimson.

Juno (*dentata superba*), about the best white night-bloomer, from Sierra Leone. Stamens bright yellow, flowers very large (up to 12in).

O'Marana, deep pink at petal base, becoming lighter towards the tip; faint white line running down the centre of each; stamens orange; foliage green with wavy margins.

OTHER TENDER AQUATICS

Ceratopteris WATER FERN; WATER SPRITE

The genus gives us the only true water ferns, delightful plants much used for aquarium work.

C. thalictroides, the Water Sprite, is really beautiful grown submerged, the dainty parsley-like leaves adding greatly to the charm of the aquaria. In shallow water and a good light they grow rapidly. I have seen them as much as 4ft long under such conditions in the Botanic Gardens at Upsala.

C. pteridoides is more floating, hence the name Floating Fern, and carries broad leaves of a pea-green colour. These are viviparous, the young plantlets being plentifully produced at the leaf-margins.

Colocasia antiquorum JAPANESE TARO; ELEPHANT'S EAR

Tuberous aroids with striking foliage, suitable for shallow water or bog cultivation. The cordate leaves, shaped something like the ear of an African elephant, may be green, purplish or mottled with green and black according to variety. The yellow arum flowers have an unpleasant odour and the stems are purplish. Tropical Asia. Propagation by division in spring.

Cyperus papyrus (syn *Papyrus antiquorum*) EGYPTIAN
PAPER PLANT

The source of papyrus, first writing paper known to the
world, and the so-called 'rushes' which are supposed to have
sheltered the infant Moses. It grows extensively along the
banks of the Nile, frequently reaching 12 to 16ft in height.

The genus is an extensive one, comprising over 400
species, but there is little doubt that *C. papyrus* is the most
striking and ornamental. One or two plants in the indoor
pool add greatly to the interest, and the graceful habit
softens the rather overpowering leaf vegetation of some
aquatics, such as nelumbo. It is best grown in a large pot
stood just under the water surface, for then the roots are
confined and prevented from spreading. The stems grow
upright, producing feathery heads of grassy inflorescence,
perfectly round and reminiscent of a large household mop.
Seed is freely produced and may be sown in shallow pans,
or a 'mop-head' may be removed and pegged into a pan of
loam and shallow water. Young plantlets will grow whilst
still attached to the head, and may be detached later. It is
also possible to divide the roots in spring.

Eichhornia crassipes major (syn *E. speciosa*) WATER
HYACINTH

A beautiful floating aquatic of unique form. In tropical
rivers it becomes a great nuisance on account of the rapid-
ity of reproduction, but in this country the slightest touch
of frost spells destruction. The buoyancy of the plant is
effected by means of the leaf petioles, which are rounded
and swollen to a considerable degree and contain much
spongy parenchyma tissue. A section cut through one of
these leaf-stalks reveals a patterning of enlarged cells somewhat reminiscent of certain types of chocolate bars. The
rounded leaves are arranged on these swollen footstalks in

circular fashion with the long purplish roots trailing down into the water. The aquarist finds goldfish partial to such appendages for spawning purposes, and is able to remove the eggs when laid, away from the parents' attentions.

The flowers are borne on a spike with 2in florets of a lavender-blue shade, each having a prominent gold mark on the upper petal. Unfortunately each bloom lasts only a day, but, in a warm house, a succession may be maintained during the summer months. Propagation is effected by means of stolons and the plants do best in shallow water and a good light. Grown close to the glass, the petioles are rounded and squat, but away from the light there is a tendency for them to 'draw', and they may reach 2ft or more in height.

Another eichhornea grown by aquarists is *E. azurea*, a species with smaller but more intensely blue flowers. The mode of growth is dissimilar, inasmuch as the plant is less compact and has a scrambling habit which carries it right across the tank. The underwater foliage of this plant is very attractive, being arranged like a succession of 'baby-ribbon' lengths up the stem. It is much used on the Continent for tropical aquaria and raised from seed and then propagated by taking cuttings. By this means it is not allowed to develop normal leaves and flowers.

Euryale ferox GORGON PLANT

A striking water-lily-like plant rarely seen in cultivation, which was, until the introduction of Victoria, thought to be the largest aquatic. Cultural requirements are identical with those of tropical nymphaeas, but the plant needs a good deal of room. The rounded leaves are about 3ft across all ways, very puckered, glowing violet beneath with thorns on the veins on both upper and under surfaces. The flowers are also deep violet, not over-large—about 2 by 3in.

Each has four very spiky sepals wrapping the corolla. The Chinese are reputed to have cultivated the plant for upwards of 3,000 years, and they eat the seeds. It is perennial and native to India.

Lasia spinosa

A curious aroid suitable for growing in shallow water. The leaves are large and very deeply cut, sometimes $2\frac{1}{2}$ by $1\frac{1}{2}$ft, with prickles up the stems and backs of the veins. The spathe of the arum-like flower may be 6 to 10in long with the upper part rolled into a tail-like extension. Tropical Asia.

Limnobium stoloniferum (syn Trianea bogotensis)

A floating plant from tropical America with thick rounded leaves heavily coated on the undersurfaces with spongy tissue. The blooms are insignificant, being white and spider-like; male and female flowers are on separate plants. A warm humid atmosphere is necessary, as under cold conditions the foliage turns brown and rots off. Increase by division.

Limnocharis flava

A coarse-growing aquatic sometimes seen in botanic gardens, but without much to commend it. It thrives best in shallow water and produces lettuce-like leaves of a very pale green, patterned and veined something like alisma. The flowers, borne in clusters of from 6 to 12in, are too pale in colour to be striking; they are pale yellow, bordered with white. Propagated by seed or division.

Nelumbium nucifera (syn Nelumbium speciosum) SACRED LOTUS

The Hindu Lotus is one of two plants associated with

Egyptian religion in ancient times—the other being *Nymphaea caerulea*. The attractive flowers and foliage and edible qualities of seed and tuber have long been known to man; the genus is indelibly linked with the cult of Buddhism. It was in the heart of a nelumbo that Brahma was thought to have been born, and the perennial nature and rise to faultless beauty from a miry environment suggested to primitive man regeneration and purification.

The magnificent glaucous-green leaves, swaying like round umbrellas on 5 to 6ft stems, are fascinating to watch in rainy weather. The drops of water roll from them like quicksilver and the oily surface never becomes wet. The large flowers are rounded and peony-like. Each bloom lasts about three days, commencing life a soft rose and deepening in colour with age. The seed pod resembles nothing so much as the rose of a watering-can; each hole containing an edible nut which eventually enlarges to the size of an acorn.

The white fleshy rootstocks need to be confined and must have a deep, rich-growing material. Cow-manure, well rotted, or coarse bonemeal make the best fertiliser, and the rhizomes should be planted just below soil-level. They need warmth (60° to 65° F.) to produce flowers, but I have grown them satisfactorily in oak tubs in a cold house.

There are many varieties of the type with white, reddish-purple and single or double flowers. The American species *pentapetalum (lutea)*, known as the Water Chinkapin or Duck Acorn, is hardier than *N. nucifera*, but the flowers are less spectacular, being a pale shade of sulphur yellow.

Neptunia oleracea (N. plena) WATER SENSITIVE

A warm-water aquatic of great charm with opposite pairs of finely pinnate leaves, reminiscent of *Mimosa pudica*. Like that plant they are sensitive to the touch. Spongy tissue on the undersurface of the stems gives the plant buoyancy, so that the habit is to lie floating on the water and scramble along the surface. Flowers are freely produced and are so heavily fringed as to have a fragile appearance; they are yellow and brown. Tropical Asia. Propagated by slips.

Nymphoides indica (syn *Limnanthemum indicum*) WATER SNOWFLAKE

One of the most charming of the smaller floating aquatics, with diminutive heart-shaped leaves resting on the surface, and clusters of inch-wide, fringed white flowers. These look like stars cut out of Turkish towelling and are unbelievably dainty. The plant thrives best in shallow water over a loam compost, and needs plenty of light, Propagated by division.

Oryza sativa RICE

The common rice of commerce is an interesting grass for the indoor pool, and the gardener may care to try a few plants. It reaches anything from 5 to 12ft in height, according to compost and temperature, with typical grassy leaves and inflorescence. Old World tropics. Propagated from seed.

Riccia CRYSTALWORT

The species *R. fluitans* and *R. natans* are floating plants forming masses of star-shaped bodies at the water-surface and collect in thick wedges several inches in depth. They are most useful for fish breeders for ova depositories, as hiding-places for the fry, and as oxygenators. The genus is native to the eastern states of North America.

Saccharum officinarum SUGAR CANE

Another interesting aquatic of economic significance

which may be cultivated in shallow water in the indoor pool. Under congenial conditions it may reach 8 to 10ft in height in this country, with grassy leaves and a dense woolly spike of inflorescence. Eastern Asia. Propagated by seed or division.

Salvinia

Small floating fern-like aquatic with heart-shaped, softly downy leaves. These are arranged in closely touching opposite pairs and look like small pieces of plush connected with threads. They quickly increase and cover the top of a warm-water aquarium. Kinds grown are *auriculata, natans* and *braziliensis.*

Typhonodorum lindleyanum

A most striking plant for deep water with robust growth and the habit of zantedeschia. The stout, smooth stems may be anything from 4 to 12in round and grow 4 to 10ft high. The leaves are deeply cordate or triangular, 1 to 3ft long and 6 to 20in across. The flowers are typical aroids, yellow, and may be up to 2ft in length. Even the seeds are large, $1\frac{3}{4}$ to 2in across; they are edible. Tropical Africa.

CHAPTER IX

Livestock for the Pool

WHILST it is not essential that livestock should be kept in the pool, most gardeners appreciate the added interest which a few fish can bring. Their presence lends animation to the scene, gives colour and movement, and plays a part in keeping down natural enemies of water plants and lilies. They also wage relentless war on one disturber of mankind—the mosquito—for it is in still waters that these pests breed and spend their larval existence.

There are several fish which may be accommodated in the garden pool—minnows, carp, tench, goldfish, golden orfe, rudd, bitterling, sticklebacks, etc, and many of them will live in harmony.

It is, however, undesirable to introduce sticklebacks, sunfish or catfish to a community pond, since these species are of pugnacious disposition and will pursue and wound the more docile inmates. Fish are natural bullies, and it is most unwise to put very small, valuable fish in with rather large coarse ones—whatever the breed. So shameless indeed are they, that they even devour their own young if given opportunity. The pond owner, therefore, should have plenty of plants in his pond, especially submerged aquatics, to provide sanctuary and cover. Shade is necessary for fish too; floating leaves provide this in summer, but a few overhanging rocks at the pond edge or one or two large hollowed pieces placed in the water will afford some protection from the sun's rays at other times.

Some water gardeners like the water clear, and these must beware of tench, carp and other 'mud dwellers'. Such species have a habit of rolling in the mud at the bottom of the pond and consequently are rarely seen, but, worse still, they keep the water in a continual muddied condition. If these types are particularly wanted, an inch layer of shingle should be placed over any soil in the pond. Even then the natural deposits from leaves, dust, etc, will gradually make a fresh layer which will be disturbed.

The most satisfactory types of fish from the gardener's point of view are the goldfish and its varieties, and golden orfe. These are brightly coloured, easily domesticated, and frequently appear at the water surface.

It is said that the famous courtesan Madame Pompadour first introduced goldfish into Europe. Even if this is true it seems certain that the centuries long patience of Oriental breeders was mainly responsible for the wide range of shapes, forms and types found in this group today. *Carassius auratus* from Korea, China and Japan has mutated and been bred into kinds with sleek bodies, new colours or enlarged and sometimes grotesque fins, tails and eyes. Some of these are slow moving and consequently less hardy than others. These are best used in aquaria or transferred from the open pond to fish tanks under cover during the winter months.

Toughest and most reliable are the so called European goldfish (*Carassius carassius*) and comets.

At one time transportation of fish involved much mortality due to overcrowding in cans and the purge which preceded travel. Nowadays they are put into plastic bags (supported inside a cardboard container) with very little water. The air is removed from the bag and replaced with pure oxygen; a manoeuvre which enables the fish to breath and exist without discomfort for approximately 48 hours. During this time they can be transported hundreds of miles. On arrival at their destination the bag should be floated on the pool (without opening) for 15-20 minutes, then unsealed so that the fish can swim out. The less they are handled the better.

Young goldfish start life olive green or black and develop to pearl, silver, yellow or gold; a few may remain dark all their lives.

An attractive hardy goldfish type is the Calico or Shubunkin, a variety which depends for its popularity upon the wonderful mottled coloration of its body. The scales are very tiny and transparent (hence it is known as a scaleless fish), and the colours it displays go through all shades of black, gold, blue, mauve, cream and red.

Another hardy variety is known as the Comet because of its streamlined body and long, straight tail. It will live happily with both the above types.

The more exotic types of goldfish, however—the black Moor, the Telescope with protruding eyes, the Celestial, whose optical organs are distorted to the extent of looking upwards the whole time, the Oranda and Lionhead, with large heads covered with wart-like excrescences, and the graceful Fantails and Veiltails—are too delicate to remain in the pond during the winter months. Since it is labourious to empty the pool each autumn to round them up, most people keep such pets in the aquarium or indoor pool the whole time.

The golden orfe is very hardy: it prefers cold water and is less subject to disease than the goldfish. It usually swims in shoals near the surface and so can be readily seen, but rarely breeds in this country. Golden orfe grow to a good length (12 to 15in) and have a long pencil-shaped body. There is a silvered variety known as silver orfe.

The British minnow is sometimes caught in the wild and added to the pond; it is a small creature, rarely exceeding 4in in length, but is lively and interesting to watch.

Other native fish, such as green tench, roach, rudd, etc, are useful in deep shady pools to keep down mosquito larvae, but, since they stir up the mud, should be barred from the ornamental pool. Dace like running water; bitterling carp are interesting in the aquaria, but too small to attract notice in the pond, and sticklebacks should be kept strictly to themselves.

The gudgeon is a scavenger and another mud stirrer, and the North American catfish also scavenges, but has an annoying habit of nipping at other fish which does not improve their appearance. There are several varieties of carp —leather carp, mirror carp, king carp, common carp, and golden carp, the latter closely resembling the common goldfish. Most of them grow to a large size and are inclined to keep to the bottom of the water.

The feeding of these pets often perplexes the newcomer to water gardening: opinions varying from the person who never feeds them at all to the kind who believes in three meals daily. In large ponds there is often a good deal of natural food, mosquito and other fly larvae, water fleas, etc. to enable a limited number of fish to survive indefinitely. In small artificial ponds, however, supplementary feeding is necessary for growth and survival.

Live food is invaluable, especially in spring and autumn. In the latter period the fish build up bodily reserves for the winter, accumulating a layer of fat which tides them over the cold periods when feeding comes practically to a standstill. During the winter months they become extremely lethargic and are scarcely seen unless a bright day tempts them to the surface. By spring their condition will be poor following the long fast period, and it is at this time of the year that fish frequently succumb to disease. It is therefore important to feed heavily about March with protein and other body-building diets. Live food is again invaluable.

Best of all such materials are water fleas, the lively teeming masses of which are sometimes found in still ponds devoid of fish life. They may be collected with a net and transferred to the pond. Other live foods are bloodworms (larvae of the chironomus fly), mosquito larvae, chopped earthworms and enchytrae or whiteworms. Greenfly, blackfly, pulverised liver, flaked boiled fish, rubbed beef, dried egg, porridge and dried flies are other foods which may be interspersed with feedings of proprietary brands of prepared dried fish food.

The chief things to remember are:

    (1) Fish appreciate variety in diet.
    (2) They should not be overfed, and, generally, as much as they will eat in five minutes is enough.
    (3) They should always be fed in the same place.
    (4) During the middle of winter they should not be fed at all in the outdoor pond.

OTHER LIVESTOCK

There are 'collectors' of livestock who like to fill their pools with frogs, newts, snails, mussels, crawfish and even terrapins or water tortoises. Such zeal, however, is largely misplaced since many of these creatures prey on the others or will cause trouble in other ways. I would advise introducing nothing beyond the fish and a few snails, the latter to act as scavengers in clearing up unconsumed food and other debris. There are several kinds of which the Ramshorn (*Planorbis corneus*) and its red form (*rubra*) and the freshwater winkle (*Paludina vivipara*) are the best. The freshwater whelk (*Limnaea stagnalis*) is less dependable and will sometimes attack water-lily leaves and flowers and also tends to multiply over rapidly.

Mussels are good scavengers, but stir up the mud when 'ploughing' the bottom of the pond, and foul the water exceedingly when one dies. They are more suited to running water conditions than still.

CHAPTER X

The Bog- and Moisture-loving Perennials

MANY gardeners will not rest satisfied with the bare pool containing its various forms of water plants and livestock, but will eventually seek to beautify the surrounds with some of the more decorative moisture-loving perennials. There are many such plants, and their careful use will prolong the season of the water garden and give splashes of colour to sombre spots.

Their chief needs are freedom from drought and abundant plant food; requirements which may be jointly met by deep cultivation and the use of moisture-holding organic material in the compost. Peat is most useful in this respect; it imparts that slightly acid condition appreciated by many bog plants, and acts as a sponge in conserving moisture and liquid plant food in the soil. Its liberal incorporation in the surrounding compost will do much to retain a constant state of dampness, and an occasional overflow from the pond will help out in really arid seasons.

For convenience sake the bog garden should be kept low, otherwise it will be difficult to flood and the moisture will drain away too readily. Its ultimate appearance as a garden feature depends on informality—as in the natural state—and any effects of equal balance on all sides should be avoided. Work for colour effects; several roots of the same plant grown together will provide a bold display infinitely more impressive than the same few plants dotted at intervals round about.

In the lush conditions of the bog garden many species will seed freely under natural conditions. Primulas especially delight in such situations, and seedlings will spring readily from the rich ground surrounding the parents. They never look happier than when grown in such a manner and, beyond occasional thinning out, may be left to colonise themselves. The agency of bees will foster cross-pollination, so that, starting with a good strain, many delightful colours will soon appear in the ranks.

At the end of the season dead herbage should be cut to ground level with the herbaceous plants and the ground lightly stirred and cleaned. A mulch of really well-rotted cow manure is excellent for soil enrichment, but, failing this, peat or compost applied as a top dressing will provide both protection and food. Some of the bog- and moisture-loving perennials may be increased by seed, particularly the species. Varieties, however, should be divided or propagated from cuttings if it is desired to keep the strain true.

The following list of plants is representative of the moisture-loving perennials suitable for the garden pond surround. It is, however, by no means exhaustive, but will serve as a guide to the gardener seeking to enhance the charm of his water garden.

Aconitum MONKSHOOD; WOLFSBANE

Well-known plants with helmet-shaped, mostly blue flowers in spikes, and handsome dark-green deeply cut leaves. The whole family favours a deep, moist soil, and under dry conditions the quality of bloom is disappointing. A semi-shaded position seems to suit them best, although they will grow in full sun, providing the soil does not dry out. The rootstock is poisonous and care must be taken when planting if there are children in the household; in point of fact the drug aconite is obtained from *A. napellus*, source of the intensely toxic alkaloid aconitine. Propagation by division or seed.

One of the most attractive species is (*A. carmichaelii* (*A. fischeri*), growing 2 to 3ft with bright sky-blue flowers and shining palmate foliage. It comes from China. *A. napellus* is the best known and grows 3 to 4ft high with dark blue spikes of flowers. It has given rise to a number of varieties with white, pink and bicoloured flowers. *A. volubile* from Siberia is distinct, being of climbing habit, but is also blue, and reaches about 4ft in height.

Actaea BANEBERRY

Vigorous growing plants, useful to the gardener having shady spots to fill. The white flowers appear in spring, but the chief value of Baneberries lies in their autumn fruits, which are red, black or white, according to variety. They may be propagated by division in spring or can be raised from seed sown soon after ripening. A good rich soil gives the best results.

A. alba is the White Baneberry and grows about 12 to 18in high; the white berries have reddish footstalks. It comes from North America. *A. spicata* from Europe (including Britain) has purplish-black fruits and serrated leaves; the roots are astringent and reputed to give relief with catarrh, whilst the berries, which are poisonous, yield with alum a black dye. There is a species with scarlet fruits called *A. rubra*.

Ajuga BUGLE

Moisture loving perennials chiefly of creeping habit, useful for carpeting. *A. reptans* is the Common Bugle of the English woodlands. They are apt to become weedy when happily situated, but are easily kept in check. Propagation by division.

A genevensis grows 6 to 9in high and has spikes of thickly packed. deep blue, nettle-like flowers. The foliage is spoon-shaped, dark green, smooth and rather small. A variety of *reptans* has variegated foliage, and there is another with purplish leaves and one having white blooms.

Anagallis PIMPERNEL

A.tenella, the Bog Pimpernel, is a pretty little native well suited to those difficult patches which appear where water and soil meet. It creeps over the ground and disguises hard margins most effectively, making a dense carpet of tiny leaves spangled with soft rosy-pink flowers. Propagated by division or seed.

Anemone WINDFLOWER

A large and beautiful genus of varied uses in the garden; one or two being suited to the bog garden.

A.rivularis is a most striking representative from the Himalayas which deserves to be much more widely known. Growing about 2ft high, it has handsome palmately divided leaves and umbels of white flowers which have violet-blue anthers.

A.virginiana comes from eastern North America and is not even damaged by occasional flooding. It is a hairy plant with 2 to 3ft stems carrying white or greenish flowers about $1\frac{1}{2}$in across under favourable conditions. It should be left undisturbed if possible, and is increased by division or seed.

Aruncus GOAT'S BEARD

A. dioicus is an old garden plant usually grown as *A. sylvester* or *Spiraea arunceus*. All the spiraeas now, however, are shrubs and the herbaceous members of the genus have been dispersed to other genera. The species is a noble waterside plant and will thrive in sunny, shaded or half-shaded situations. It needs a rich, deep soil, constantly moist, and when so provided produces handsome 4ft stems carrying large corymbs of creamy-white flowers, and long lanceolate, deeply cut leaves. It makes a good cut flower and is normally in bloom about June to July. One plant, when established, will cover an area about 3ft square. It comes from Siberia and North America. There is a form known as *kneiffii*, lower growing (3ft) with foliage so finely cut that it looks almost fern-like.

Aruncus dioicus, a handsome waterside plant with creamy-white flowers

Arundinaria BAMBOO

There are a number of hardy bamboos, eminently suited to the proximity of water. The most commonly cultivated are *Phyllostachys, Sinarundinaria, Arundinaria, Pleioblastus* and *Pseudosasa* species and forms.

The plants need a deep rich loamy soil and benefit considerably from a mulch of rotted organic material in the spring. They must not be allowed to become dry, particularly during the first few years, and most of them resent cutting winds. A watchful eye should be kept on the running kinds so that they do not outgrow their original positions. Propagation is best effected by division in April or May, retaining a ball of soil round the roots if possible.

A. anceps needs a warm, sheltered position. It grows 10 to 12ft high, and has fairly narrow leaves.

A. japonica (originally *Bambusa metake*, now correctly known as *Pseudosasa japonica*) is the commonest of the hardy bamboos and makes a good screen as the foliage is evergreen. It is readily distinguished by the broad glossy leaves and from the brownish sheaths enwrapping the stem. It may be recommended for town gardens. Japan.

A. murielae (now referred to *Sinarundinaria*) makes a good 'dot' plant, for it does not run. Growing 10ft high, the arching wands are profusely clothed with narrow tapering leaves. It closely resembles *A. nitida*, except that the latter plant is more upright in growth. Both come from China.

A. simonii (now referred to *Pleioblastus*). One of the tallest of the genus, frequently reaching 10 to 20ft. Broad, vivid foliage, tapering to a fine point and frequently striped with white. China.

Arundo REED

Elegant grasses for sheltered positions in deep rich soil. *A. donax* comes from southern Europe and reaches from 10 to 20ft according to locality. The stout glaucous leaves are very ornamental, although less so than the variegated forms var *macrophylla* and var *versicolor*.

Asclepias MILKWEED

Easily grown plants with no special requirements, suitable for the wild parts of the garden although some make good border plants.

A. incarnata is the Swamp Milkweed, found in North American swamps. It grows about 3 to 3½ft tall, with stout leafy stems and umbels of rosy pink flowers in July and August. There is a variety *alba* with white flowers and another *pulchra* having dull red ones. Increased by division in spring.

Aster MICHAELMAS DAISY

Few members of this family are really suited to the bog garden, but there are one or two North American species which naturally come from a marsh environment and might be included in the wet parts of the garden.

A. junceus is the Rush Aster, a slender species 2 to 3ft high, with grassy leaves and violet or white flowers. It will grow in real bogland or even in shallow water.

A. nemoralis, the Bog Aster, is lower growing (6 to 24in), but a better plant with heavy heads of large blue or pink flowers.

A. paludosus is the Southern Swamp Aster from eastern North America and grows 18 to 30in tall with rough leaves and deep violet flowers.

A. puniceus makes a good swamp plant and is quite hardy. It has reddish stems with violet-blue flowers. Height, 3 to 5ft.

A. tripolium, the Sea Aster, is a native of our salt marshes with small purplish flowers, but is not very ornamental.

Astilbe

A genus to be remembered by the aquatic gardener, for the whole family likes plenty of water during the growing season. They will grow in sun or shade providing only that sufficient moisture is available; and it will be found that the incorporation of peat or leaf-mould in the compost does much to prevent drying-out in arid situations. In heavy soils it is wise to defer planting until spring. Propagation is best effected by division at this time.

The charm of the plants lies in their feathery (spiraea-like) plumes of flowers, variously coloured in white, pink, purple or red, and the handsome compound leaves. The forms usually grown are of hybrid origin, collectively grouped under the trade name of *Astilbe arendsii*. They normally flower from July to August, and for best effects must be planted in groups. Typical varieties of *A. arendsii* are 'Amethyst', violet-purple, 4ft; 'Avalanche', white, 3ft;

Astilbe 'Fanal' and 'Emden' growing by a poolside

'Betsy Cuperus', pink and white, 5ft; 'Fanal', brilliant red-crimson, 2½ft; 'Granat', cerise, 2½ft; 'Gunther', bright pink, 3ft; and 'Silver Sheaf', silvery-white, 3ft.

Other useful astilbes include *A. crispa,* a hybrid from *A. simplicifolia,* and an *arendsii* seedling, with crinkled foliage and masses of pink and white flowers from 4 to 6in high, and *A. davidii,* a Chinese species, 4 to 6ft tall, with coarsely palmate leaves and 2ft panicles of rosy purple flowers.

A. japonica, from Japan, has broad three-parted leaves and heavy plumes of white flowers. It is frequently used for forcing and grows 1 to 3ft tall.

A. rivularis has a dainty habit with deeply divided leaves and spires of creamy-white flowers. It is of creeping habit, and native to brooks and waterways in western China.

A. simplicifolia is a dwarf form from Japan with glossy foliage and short (9in) panicles of flowers. The type is white, but there are a number of hybrids with variously coloured spikes.

Astrantia MASTERWORT

Although not outstanding from the colour point of view, the Masterworts have some adherents amongst those who appreciate the oddities of plant life. The umbels of pink, rose or white flowers are surrounded by pale green bracts, which turn purplish later, whilst the foliage is lobed and the rootstock somewhat aromatic. They require a modicum of shade in moist soil and show some partiality for lime. Propagated by division of the roots in spring or autumn. The chief kinds grown are *A. carniolica,* 1ft, and *A. major,* 2 to 3ft.

Buphthalmum

B. speciosum (*Telekia speciosa*) is a robust plant more

suited to the wild garden than small formal sites. It grows 4 to 5ft high, with large yellow daisy flowers with dark eyes, and heart-shaped, coarsely toothed leaves. It spreads rapidly by means of underground runners. Increased by division in spring or autumn. Europe.

Camassia

Few bulbs appreciate bog conditions in the garden, but the North American camassias are frequently under water at flowering time in their native habitat. They should be planted 3 to 5in deep in a rich moist soil and left undisturbed.

C. leichtlinii, is a vigorous species growing 3ft high, with large creamy-white flowers on stout spikes. British Columbia.

C. quamash, 2ft, dark blue. Western North America.

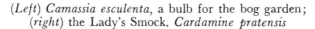

(*Left*) *Camassia esculenta*, a bulb for the bog garden; (*right*) the Lady's Smock. *Cardamine pratensis*

Cardamine

The common Lady's Smock (*C. pratensis*) is a well-known denizen of wet meadowland, a delicate jewel of fragile and fleeting beauty. Its double form *fl pl* is a better garden plant, more compact with a sturdier spike of flowers. Growing about 1ft high, the lilac-pink flowers are reminiscent of a miniature double stock and bloom most freely in shaded places from May to June. Propagated by division.

Chamaenerion (Epilobium) FIRE WEED; ROSE BAY

Showy but weedy plants, only suited to wild garden culture. In the dim corners of close knit woodland or in stretches of waste land unsuited to choicer plants, the bright rose spikes of the Fire Weed shine like beacons. The type is *C. angustifolium*, but there is a white form, *album*, and a most attractive soft pink variety called Isabel which has received the Award of Merit of the R.H.S. It is less inclined to seed and more readily kept in bounds than the others. Height, 2 to 5ft, according to variety. Increased by underground runners or seed.

Chelone TURTLE-HEAD

These curious North American perennials get their common name from the grotesque snapdragon-like heads. They are hardy and happy under boggy conditions, and fill a want inasmuch as they bloom in late summer. There are three sorts grown in this country—*C. glabra*, with white or blush-tinted flowers, 2ft; *C. lyonii*, reddish-purple, heart-shaped leaves, 2 to 3ft; and *C. obliqua*, reddish-purple, 2ft, the first one to flower.

Chrysanthemum

A well-known genus with few aquatic representatives. *C. lacustre*, from Portugal, is, however, a good plant for the boggy parts of the wild garden. Its white blooms are reminiscent of the Marguerite Daisy (*C. maximum*) and may be used for cutting. It grows 2ft high.

C. uliginosum is another swamp chrysanthemum and in lush conditions reaches 4 to 5ft in height. The flowers are white, about 3in across, very late in the season (September to October), when most other plants have passed. Propagation by division.

Cimicifuga BUGBANE

A group of plants with handsome divided foliage and spikes of astilbe-like flowers, suitable for the drier parts of the water garden. They favour some shade—that dappled light which one gets under trees—and in well-cultivated soil provide a pleasing display in late summer. Propagation is effected by division of the roots in spring or autumn.

C. americana has heart-shaped foliage and sends up strong 4ft stems bearing very many small white flowers arranged in spikes. North America.

C. dahurica grows a little taller than the preceding and has blackish stems and creamy white flowers. Manchuria.

C. racemosa has white feathery spikes borne in branching profusion from August until late September. It grows 3 to 8ft high, according to conditions, and has handsome dark-green leaves. A variety known as 'Avalanche' is an improvement on the type. North America.

The variety *simplex* is 3ft tall, with more compact and unbranched spires of similar flowers.

Claytonia SPRING BEAUTY

Dwarf plants with bright green, almost succulent leaves, and a creeping, spreading, irrepressible habit when happily situated. They make useful carpeters in the wild garden or damp woodland. Increased by seed or division.

C. sibirica has pale pink, five-petalled flowers, lightly striated with carmine. Height, 6in. June to September. Siberia.

C. virginica, from North America, has small linear leaves spangled with white flowers tinged pink. 2 to 6in.

Coptis trifolia GOLD-THREAD

A creeping evergreen with shining three-parted leaves and slender scapes of small white flowers. It grows no more than 3 to 6in and makes an unusual carpeter for the shady parts of the bog garden. Propagated by division. North America.

Coreopsis TICKSEED

The only species of this ubiquitous genus suited to the water garden is *C. rosea,* a North American wilding growing 12 to 18in high. It has narrow grassy foliage and quantities of inch-wide, deep-rose, daisy-like flowers with golden discs. Propagated by division in spring.

Cypripedium LADY'S SLIPPER

Although temperamental, the hardy slipper orchids are amongst the most beautiful of plants for the bog garden, and well worth a trial. They need a position shaded throughout the day but receiving the evening sun, and like a moist, but not waterlogged, peaty soil. The roots must be well spread out, and the plants top-dressed annually with peat or leaf-mould. Once established they are best left undisturbed. Propagated by division in autumn.

C. candidum flowers in May and June and reaches 6 to 12in in height. The blooms are green and brown on the sepals with a white 'pouch' striped inside with purple. North America.

C. calceolus var *pubescens.* About 22in tall. Flowers

Cypripedium reginae, a hardy slipper orchid, flowering in June

April to May, large brown pouches flecked with purple and twisted yellowish-green sepals. North America.

C. japonicum, 18in high. Flowers greenish or silvery-white spotted crimson. April to May. Japan.

C. reginae (syn *C. spectabile*). A showy species with a white, crimson overlaid pouch and pure white sepals. Height, 12 to 18in. Flowering in June, this handsome plant comes to us from the tamarix and cedar swamps of North America.

Epigaea repens TRAILING ARBUTUS

An attractive little evergreen for shady spots, it is allergic to lime, but happily suited by acid, peaty soil conditions. It spreads in such instances with an insidious creeping habit, producing dense patches of dark green leaves and clusters of white or rose-tinted flowers. Propagated by seed, division or layers.

Eupatorium HEMP AGRIMONY

Coarse perennials with sufficient individuality to merit the attention of the bog gardener. They will grow in almost any type of soil, but attain finer proportions in damp, marshy ground or at the waterside. They are propagated by division.

E. cannabinum is the Hemp Agrimony of Europe (including Britain). A tall, downy plant, it grows 3 to 6ft high, with large palmately divided leaves, reddish stems and imposing plate like inflorescences—made up of many small, dull purple flowers. There is a double form which is more impressive.

E. purpureum, from North America, is known in that country as the Joe Pye Weed and grows to 6 to 8ft, with branching heads of crimson-purple flowers in open, plate-like heads.

Filipendula DROPWORT; MEADOWSWEET

A beautiful genus (formerly associated with the spiraeas, but now kept distinct) which delights in the moist, rich soil of the waterside and a sunny or semi-shaded situation. They are aptly suited to riverside planting in positions where the feathery sprays of inflorescence may be advantageously reflected in the water. They may be increased by seed or division in spring.

F. hexapetala (*Spiraea filipendula*) is the Dropwort and has fern-like leaves and upright heads of fragrant creamy flowers. 1 to 3ft. Europe, including Britain. There is a double form.

F. purpurea (*Spiraea palmata*), from Japan, is a first-rate water-side perennial with deep purplish tresses of flowers in late summer. There is a white form. Height, 2 to 4ft.

F. rubra (*Spiraea lobata*), a fine North American species with large palmate leaves and feathery plumes of fragrant rosy flowers. Var *venusta* is deep pink. Height, 2 to 5ft.

F. ulmaria (*Spiraea ulmaria*), although rarely planted by design, our native Meadowsweet makes a handsome wild garden subject with its showy fragrant feathery plumes. The double form is more widely cultivated and has masses of double sweet-scented, creamy flowers arranged in feathery trails. The buds are reddish, which adds to the flower's charm. Height, 3ft. July to August.

Fritillaria

A large and interesting genus, most of which favour a sandy, peaty soil with plenty of water during the growing season. In wet meadowland, *F. meleagris*, the Snake's Head Fritillary, with curious hanging, chequer-board-patterned flowers of purple and white, and with its white variety, *alba,* may be naturalised with advantage. They should be left undisturbed to form large colonies. Height, 1ft. April to May. Europe, Asia.

Geum WATER AVENS

Good garden plants for general use, one species, *G. rivale*, suited to the water garden. It attains a height of about 1ft, with strawberry-like leaves and nodding heads of terra-cotta red in purple calyces, which are in bloom almost the whole year round. It has thrown several varieties, including *album*, white, and 'Leonard's var', old rose. Europe, including Britain.

Gunnera

Imposing waterside subjects for the large garden.

G. manicata has enormous rhubarb-like leaves on prickly stems and yard-long inflorescences of green and brown which resemble nothing so much as a bottle brush. I have known the leaves attain dimensions of 10 by 7ft in one season. Frost is fatal to the plant, and immediately it kills the foliage in autumn, the leaves should be cut off and inverted over the crown to form a natural mulch and protection. Ample moisture at the roots at all times and an occasional mulch with rotted manure or compost are its chief requirements. Propagated by division.

G. manicata, 8 to 10ft tall, and will cover an area of 20 sq ft in a few years, so must be given plenty of room. Brazil.

G. chilensis (*scabra*), a slightly smaller plant requiring similar cultivation, and having reddish hairs on the stems and more reddish flowers. 6ft. Chile.

Helonias STUD-FLOWER; SWAMP PINK

A monotypic genus, the species *H. bullata* being a handsome North American bog perennial with spikes of purplish-pink flowers and close rosettes of shiny dark green foliage. Height, 1 to 2ft. Propagated by division.

Hemerocallis DAY-LILY

Ideal waterside plants, although the genus is as adaptable as any in the vegetable kingdom and there are few spots where they will not grow. Once established, the clumps may be left undisturbed for many years, and the golden, yellow or orange flowers will appear at intervals all the summer. The narrow grassy foliage is neat and compact and grows closely enough to give some measure of control to weeds. There are a number of species, such as *aurantiaca*, orange-yellow, Japan, 3ft; *flava*, China, 3ft; and *fulva*, reddish orange, 3½ft, temperate Asia. The form 'Kwanso' of the latter species has double flowers and var *rosea* gives colour by virtue of its soft rose blooms. Nowadays, however, there are many hybrids to choose from—from 15in to 4½ft tall, early blooming and late, and forms with orange, red, bronze, gold, yellow and striated flowers. The study of a nursery-man's catalogue will give varieties to suit all tastes. Propagated by division.

Heracleum COW PARSNIP

H. villosum (syn *H. giganteum*) is one of those grotesque plants which have to be seen to be believed. At the water-side or in a damp spot in the wild garden it will grow 8 to 12ft high, with parsnip-like leaves and enormous plate-like heads, up to 18in across, covered with small white flowers. It seeds very readily and may become a nuisance unless watched. Caucasus.

Hosta PLANTAIN LILY

A group of fine-foliaged, shade-loving plants, invaluable for woodland or waterside planting. A deep rich loam, un-likely to dry out, suits them best, and once established they should be left undisturbed. The flowers, mauve or white, are of secondary importance to the leaves, which may be variegated, fluted, ribbed or of a green or steely-blue colour. The family is often referred to as funkia. Propagation by division.

H. decorata, often called Thomas Hogg, has dull, dark green leaves, white-margined with dark lilac flowers. Japan.

H. fortunei, heart-shaped, glaucous foliage (8 by 6½in), and lilac blooms. Japan. *Albo-picta* is variegated.

H. sieboldiana, (H. glauca) big cordate leaves (14 by 10in), very glaucous and ribbed, lilac flowers. Japan.

H. undulata, twisted leaves, heavily variegated in white, lilac flowers. Japan.

Hosta fortunei albo-picta,
a shade-loving Plantain
Lily

H. undulata var *erromena,* forms large clumps of dark green leaves and pale lilac flowers.

Inula ELACAMPANE

Showy composites suited to moist ground in the wild garden. *I. glandulosa* is a dwarf (2ft) with saffron-yellow daisy heads and comes from the Caucasus.

I. helenium bears ragged yellow sunflowers, about 3in across, and grows 3 to 5ft tall. It is a British plant.

I. royleana, from the Himalayas, is the best of the genus, with black buds which open to very large, bright orange daisies of striking appearance. Height, 2ft. June to September. Propagated by division or seed.

Iris

Some of the most beautiful waterside plants come in this

genus, and bold clumps of the various species give imposing effects. A rich moist soil is appreciated by the moisture-loving forms, but no lime must be given. Most of them are propagated by division in spring.

I. aurea, a robust plant from the Himalayas, bearing imposing rich golden flowers on 4 to 5ft stems about July. The foliage is exceptionally broad and tough.

I. bulleyana, from China, grows 18 to 30in high, with grassy leaves and rich blue flowers.

I. delavayi comes from China and likes a marshy site. Under favourable conditions it will reach 5ft, with very long, sword-shaped, grey-green leaves and brilliant violet and white flowers.

I. forrestii, also from China, is creamy yellow, and likes a reasonably moist or half-shaded site. 18in. June.

I. kaempferi, the clematis-flowered iris of Japan, gay as butterflies on the wing, but temperamental. Their real requirements are plenty of water during the growing season and comparative dryness in winter—not always easy. A retentive soil made up of leaf or peat gives some semblance of this condition, and full sun is to be preferred. The flowers of some are selfs—blues, pinks, reds and white—and of others, in various mixtures of shades. They usually have Japanese names.

I. laevigata, see p. 57.

I. sibirica, excellent waterside subjects with narrow, grassy leaves and slender stems carrying mauve, blue or white flowers. These are frequently fragrant and good for cutting. Good varieties are Caesar, 3ft, violet-purple; Perry's Blue, 4ft, sky-blue; Snow Queen, 2ft, white; China Blue, 3ft, soft blue; and Tropic Night, 2ft, almost black.

I. versicolor, grey-green leaves, purplish-blue flowers variegated with yellow, green and white. 2ft. North America.

Kirengeshoma

K. palmata is an unusual but attractive plant with large, wide, jagged leaves and soft yellow, bell-shaped flowers, borne in loose sprays. August to September, 2 to 4ft. Japan.

Lobelia

These aristocrats of the waterside are not nearly as well known as they deserve, as for brilliance of colouring they stand alone. It is true that winter spells the death knell of some forms, but these may be over-wintered in cold frames and replanted in spring. Propagation by division or soft cuttings in spring.

L. cardinalis grows to 3ft in height, with smooth, polished leaves and sealing-wax scarlet, salvia-like flowers. August to October. North America.

L. fulgens, from Mexico, is somewhat similar, but with larger and more showy flowers and bronze foliage. There are also many fine horticultural forms, such as 'Huntsman', scarlet; 'Jack MacMasters', violet-blue with purple foliage;

Lobelia cardinalis, a scarlet waterside flower growing to 3ft

'Riverside', petunia-purple; 'Purple Emperor', rich purple; and 'Rose Gem', bright rose.

L. syphilitica, a North American species with bright purple flowers. 18in. July to August; var *alba* is a white form.

Lysichitum

A genus of two plants suited to a damp corner in the water garden. Here they should be left to naturalise, to present imposing effects in spring with huge yellow or white arum-like flowers, and later attract attention with 4ft by 15in coarse glaucous leaves.

L. americanum has yellow blooms, North American, and *L. camtschatcense* white ones. Japan.

Lysimachia

Moisture loving plants, best grown where the sunlight is interrupted, or in the wild garden. They are propagated by division.

L. clethroides, from Japan, has attractive spikes of pure white primrose-like flowers on 2 to 3ft high stems. The large broadly lanceolate leaves colour in autumn.

L. thyrsiflora, a rare native with axillary heads of yellow flowers which will actually grow right in the water. Height, 1 to 3ft.

L. vulgaris, a showy native for the wild garden, 2 to 3ft high, with tapering leaves and terminal panicles of large yellow flowers.

Lythrum PURPLE LOOSESTRIFE

Ideal subjects for massing in wild garden settings. They all thrive in a wet soil and bring pleasing flashes of colour to sombre spots. Propagation by division.

L. salicaria is a native plant with reddish-purple flowers on 3ft spikes; it is less widely grown than some of the garden forms, such as *atropurpureum*, rich dark purple; 'Brightness', clear pink; 'Lady Sackville', vivid rose-purple; and 'The Beacon', rose-red. To see the setting sun behind a clump of lythrums makes an unforgettable picture—the flowers seem to glow as if on fire.

Mimulus MUSK

A showy genus of moisture-loving annuals or perennials a doubtful hardiness, but which produce a dazzling array of colour for a long period. All require a constantly damp soil, such as is found at the water's edge. They grow readily from seed, but named varieties are easily raised from cuttings, and for safety's sake should be wintered indoors.

M. cardinalis, from North America, has deep scarlet flowers with yellow throats. 18in. Easily raised from seed.

(Left) Mimulus require the constantly damp soil found at the water's edge; *(right) Monarda* 'Croftway Pink', a nettle-like perennial

M. lewisii, rosy crimson; var *alba* white. North America. Flowers freely but likes a subdued light.

M. guttatus, from North America, gives us some fine garden varieties, such as 'Whitecroft's Scarlet', sealing-wax scarlet; Bees' Dazzler, scarlet; the hybrids *tigrinus, cupreus* and *maculosus*, and the Hose-in-Hose sorts which have a double corolla ring. Some will come true from seed, but all may be easily raised from cuttings.

M. ringens, also from North America, has deep lavender flowers. 2ft. June to August.

Monarda BEE BALM

Pleasantly scented, nettle-like perennials with square stems, toothed leaves, and spikes of bright flowers. Often treated as border plants, they are at home in damp soil and usually flower well in such situations. The North American *M. didyma* has thrown some fine forms, such as 'Cambridge Scarlet', 2½ft, July to August; 'Croftway Pink', rose-pink; 'Crimson King', crimson; and var *violacea purpurea*, deep rose purple.

Phormium NEW ZEALAND FLAX

Ornamental foliage plants of imposing stature, which should be given prominent positions in the water garden. Large specimens command much attention with their coarse sword-shaped leaves and rigid branching candelabras of red and yellow flowers. They are not very hardy and in exposed positions should receive light protection during the winter.

P. colensoi (syn *P. cookianum*) has leaves 2 to 5ft long with a flower scape 3 to 7ft high. There is a yellow variegated form.

P. tenax has tough leathery leaves edged with red or brown. Stout 5 to 10ft stems bear the dull red or yellow

tubular flowers. August to October. There are varieties
with reddish-purple and variegated foliage.

Podophyllum MAY-APPLE

Curious perennials favouring a moist situation and
shade.

P. emodi has large three-lobed, umbrella-like leaves and
creamy-white flowers which are succeeded by large, tomato-
like, 2in, scarlet fruits. 15in. Himalayas.

P. peltatum, 12 to 18in high, has white flowers and yellow
fruits.

P. versipelle, 3ft, twin peltate leaves and hanging crimson flowers. China.

Polygonum KNOTWEED

Coarse plants of a growth prolific enough to command
respect; some species ought never to be introduced to the
garden at all. The following kinds are decorative and may
be employed for wild garden work or in confined spots at
the waterside:

P. affine, spikes of rosy flowers. 18in. Himalayas.

P. bistorta, British, 1 to 2ft. Spikes of pale pink flowers
and dock-like leaves.

P. campanulatum, 3ft, in flower all summer with graceful sprays of heather-like bloom; leaves strongly veined,
dark green above and silvery beneath. Himalayas.

Primula PRIMROSE

A tremendous family, the majority favouring moist conditions, ie a damp soil which is not waterlogged. For
colonising they are invaluable, and no water garden can
afford to dispense with their colourful, graceful, tiered
spikes of flowers. Top dressing occasionally with well rotted
manure and leaf-mould improves the quality of the plants

and prevents drying out. Propagation by seed sown soon after gathering, or by division.

P. beesiana, from China, is one of the best moisture-loving primulas, with tiers of fragrant rosy-carmine flowers. 2ft. May to June.

P. bulleyana, also Chinese, has golden-yellow flowers with reddish buds. 2½ft. May to June.

P. denticulata, the commonest Himalayan primrose, growing 1 to 2ft tall, with globular heads of lilac flowers; there is also a white form.

P. florindae, one of the tallest species, resembles a giant cowslip, with 3ft stems of fragrant, soft yellow, hanging bells. July to August.

P. helodoxa, many tiers of rich yellow blooms on 3ft stems. China.

P. japonica, perhaps the most satisfactory group for the waterside. The type is crimson, but seed from selected varieties shows many shades of white, crimson and pink. 2ft Japan.

Primula denticulata, a common Himalayan primrose

One of the tallest of the primrose family;
Primula florindae reaches 3ft

P. pulverulenta resembles the preceding, except that the stems are mealy. Bartley strain is a selected group which gives some fine colour forms. 2½ft. China.

P. rosea, a charming little Himalayan species growing 6 to 9in high, with tufts of pale green foliage and loose umbrels of clear rose flowers in spring. It should be grown in wet soil at the waterside and left to colonise.

P. sikkimensis is the Himalayan cowslip—a beautiful plant with long, narrow leaves and slender spikes of fragrant, nodding, large pale-yellow bells. Easily raised from seed. 2ft. July to August.

Ranunculus CROWFOOT

The genus may be said to appreciate a damp position as a general rule, although there are a few genuine aquatics. Cultural requirements present no problems, a moist, friable loam and a sunny position suiting most kinds. Propagated by division or seeds.

R. aconitifolius has handsome, broadly toothed, shiny leaves and great quantities of single white flowers on branching stems. 2½ft. May to June. Europe. The double form, also known as Fair Maids of France, is the more decorative.

R. acris flore pleno is the yellow Bachelor's Buttons, with quantities of double, glossy, golden button flowers. June to August. 2ft. Europe.

Rheum RHUBARB

Handsome foliage plants of tropical luxuriance, particularly adapted to the waterside or wild garden. A single plant should be grown as a specimen for maximum effect. Plant in moist, rich soil and propagate by seed or division.

R. emodi, from the Himalayas, has bronze-green, glossy leaves with large red veins and whitish spikes of flowers. 5 to 10ft. June to July.

A. palmatum, deeply lobed, palmate leaves and spires of deep red flowers. 8 to 10ft. China. There is also a variety with more deeply dissected leaves and rich crimson flowers and fruit.

Rodgersia

Beautiful foliage plants with handsome leaves and spikes of astilbe-like flowers. They favour a damp position at the waterside and a semi-shaded light. Increased by root-cuttings or division.

R. aesculifolia, bronze-green foliage resembling that of the horse-chestnut in shape, and flat sprays of fluffy white flowers. 3ft. June to August. China.

R. pinnata, olive green leaves, much divided and branched panicles of rosy blossoms. 2 to 3ft. China. There is a white form.

R. podophylla, heavily netted, palmately divided, bronz-

The rosy-blossomed
Rodgersia pinnata

ed leaves and yellowish-white flowers. 4ft. Japan.

R. tabularis, leaves almost round, 2 to 3ft across, on very long stems; flowers creamy-white. 3ft. China.

Senecio RAGWORT

Showy plants of vigorous growth; the boggy sorts of particular value in the wild garden. Propagated by seed or division.

S. aquaticus, Marsh Ragwort. A 2ft native with coarse-toothed leaves and loose sprays of golden daisy-like flowers.

S. clivorum (now referred to the genus *Ligularia*) has large rounded, sharply toothed leaves, frequently more than a foot across and stout stems carrying crowded heads of rich orange flowers. July to September. 3ft. Japan.

S. pulcher, from South America, has reddish-purple flowers with yellow centres and long, lobed, silvery leaves. 3ft. August to October.

Sidalcea

S. *candida*, from western North America, is a representative of a well-known garden genus which may be introduced with advantage to the water garden. It grows about $3\frac{1}{2}$ft tall, with modest, white, hollyhock-like flowers on long spikes, and palmately divided buttercup-like foliage. Propagated by division. Flowers June to August.

Symplocarpus SKUNK CABBAGE

S. *foetidus* is a curious North American perennial with a most unpleasant odour when bruised and quaint 3 to 6in arum-like flowers of purple and green, very early in the year. These are succeeded by large heart-shaped leaves, 1 to 3ft long, and frequently 1ft broad. Propagated by division.

Trollius GLOBE FLOWER

Graceful subjects—relations of the buttercup—for open sunny places at the water's edge, with round ball-like heads of yellow or orange flowers. Propagated by division in spring.

There are a number of species, usually passed over in favour of the garden varieties, of which there is a wide range. These are normally 2 to 3ft tall and in flower from May to July.

Examples are: Canary Bird, pale yellow; Fire Glow, fiery orange and yellow; Juliana, deep orange; Goliath, dark orange; Orange Princess, deep yellow.

CHAPTER XI

Troubles in the Water Garden

DURING all the time the water garden has been under the process of construction the gardener has probably been spurred on by the belief that once the manual labour was completed and the planting finished, his troubles would be over. In his mind's eye he visualised beautiful water-lilies in full bloom, waving reeds, colourful bog plants and, more appealing still, a stretch of water—crystal clear and limpid. In a matter of two to four weeks he knows differently. The odds are that the pond will be dank and discoloured—resembling in fact pea soup more nearly than *aqua pura*. Desperately, in an attempt to remedy matters, he draws off the water and refills the pool, only to be faced with the same trouble a little later on.

Now this is an extreme case, but it *does* happen, so before adopting any drastic remedial measures it might be as well to consider the causes and effects of green water.

First of all, we must realise that in making a pool we have attempted to construct in a few weeks a feature which Nature would take perhaps years to effect. Everything has been rushed, the planting, pond construction (with unnatural media), new soil and tap water.

Fill a glass with water and leave it for a few days. At the end of that time there will be a decided discolouration and a thin film of mulm at the bottom. Some of this is dust, but there will also be present a vast assemblage of minute plant and animal life—a fact which can be verified with the aid of a good microscope. The organisms are living on the minute mineral particles dissolved in the water and on themselves. Similarly, in the pond the same thing is happening, only here we have as well waste products and unconsumed food from the fish, various organic materials breaking down in the compost, leaves from nearby trees, and sometimes oil seepings or such-like substances washing down from the surrounding paths, etc.

In a natural pond Nature lends a hand at flood-time by washing off a lot of this material or in summer the pond dries up and is sweetened by the action of sun and air. Oxygenation also plays a big part in clarifying the water, and it is here that we have one of the answers to the problem.

Green water takes its colour from the hosts of minute plants called algae which are thriving in it. They feed on dissolved mineral salts and otherwise grow and multiply much like other plants. When fish are present it is absolutely essential to introduce some form of plant life to maintain the oxygen content and preserve a balance. Of course algae will do this, and let us say here right away that green water such as this is *not* unhealthy; it is only unsightly. In extreme cases, of course, the thread-like algae will multiply to such an extent as to strangle other plants or enmesh small fish, but this kind is easily removed with a stick and is not the form to which we are now referring. The way to combat it in the present instance is to introduce competition. Add other plants, stronger growing and more demanding, and they will virtually starve the algae out of existence—both from the food and light point of view.

In the chapter on submerged aquatics we spoke of the wonderful way in which the green plant broke down carbon dioxide, utilising the carbon for its growing purposes and returning the oxygen to the water. All plants need the sun's energy to perform this function so that one of the first steps in the green pond must be to reduce the light. Poolside plantings of tall aquatics (especially on the sunny side), the introduction of underwater plants, strong growing lilies and floating aquatics provide shade easily and naturally. Once they become established they will take precedence in the struggle for available plant food, and the algae will starve. In newly built ponds the algal growth is naturally prolific until such times as the other plants become established. Ultimately the food upon which it thrives will diminish and its growth subside back to normal; by changing the water you merely give it a fresh lease of life.

Incidentally, there is one sure and certain way to clear green water, and that is to add daphnia; they will clear it in no time. It is no use doing this, however, if you have fish, for they eat the daphnia.

Another cause of discoloured water is too much organic material in the compost. Insufficiently rotted manure, loam which has not stood long enough in the stack, so that much of the fibrous material still remains, the introduction of fertilisers or fatty materials are all potential causes of trouble. During the disintegration of these substances chemical changes take place which temporarily alter the status of the water. Toxic substances may be emitted which could affect the well-being of plants and fish if produced in sufficient quantities. Frequently in such cases a fatty, scummy material will rise from the bottom and float on the surface. It follows that preventive measures are better than remedies, and the gardener should give good attention to this question of compost. A layer of shingle or coarse sand over the soil will prevent organic materials from coming into direct contact with the water, and is particularly valuable when bottom fish, such as carp or tench (which rub in the mulm and stir up the mud) are present. When scum does rise to the surface it should be removed with a net or run off by overflowing the pond.

Incorrectly seasoned ponds may also give trouble in the early stages of their existence, and where this is at fault remedial measures must be adopted as given in Chapter III.

Chemical methods to control algae are dangerous for the amateur. It is true that copper sulphate crystals will rid the water of it for a while, but they so impregnate the water with copper as to cause trouble in other directions and upset the normal balance. There are several proprietary substances on the market which give short term control. These can be used provided the manufacturers' instructions are strictly adhered to. Never overdo the dose in order to speed the operation.

In conclusion, then, discoloured water may be caused by:
(1) Decomposing organic material
(2) Unseasoned concrete
(3) Water adjustments plus insufficient plant life plus too much light
(4) Fish stirring up the mud

Remedies involve:
Planting some oxygenating subjects
Providing shade
Running off scum, but otherwise leaving the water alone
Seasoning the pool
Placing shingle over the mud when fish are present

WEEDS

Somebody once said that a weed was a plant in the wrong

place, and this term in the water garden might equally apply to the thread-like ropes of algae, which tangle everything as they go, as to superfluous vegetation of all kinds, below water and above. All gardeners spend half their life pulling weeds, and the pond-owner does not escape. Some of the weeds can be raked out, or fished up with a net, but most of it is work for bare hands and there are no short cuts.

PESTS AND DISEASES

WATER-LILY APHIS (*Rhopalosiphum nymphaeae*)

Several varieties of aphis attack aquatic plants, but the one mentioned is particularly troublesome and can completely ruin a stock of water-lilies. The doubtful honour of supporting it is shared by the plum, for it is on plum trees that the eggs are laid in autumn, and in spring the hatching females wing their way to the water-lilies and other aquatic plants. Here by asexual reproduction they give birth to living wingless females which in their turn repeat the process in a few days' time. Winged forms are not produced until the pest wishes to migrate, and in autumn males appear, sexual reproduction proceeds, and the eggs are laid. It follows that early detection and treatment are necessary if the pest is to be kept under control.

An application of a contact wash, such as pyrethrum extract or nicotine soap should be given as soon as possible, particularly if no livestock is present. Derris washes are poisonous to fish, and must on no account be used if these are present. Fortunately many aphides are parasitsed or destroyed by birds, and a heavy shower dislodges numbers into the water where fish devour them. A forcible spraying from a hose is efficacious, too, if there are fish present, or the energetic gardener with a very small pool can wipe them off the leaves and kill them in that way. In the aquarium they can be destroyed by cutting a piece of cardboard the size of the tank and floating this on the surface for about an hour; all the aphis will be pushed under the water and drowned.

BROWN CHINA MARKS MOTH (*Hydrocampa nymphaeata*)

Another pest of local occurrence, but troublesome to eradicate. The small dark-brown beetle (about twice the size of a ladybird) hibernates during the winter in pondside vegetation and comes on the water-lilies about June. The eggs are laid in clusters on the leaf surface and hatch out in about a week. They turn into small, slug-like creatures, very dark brown above and yellowish beneath, which feed voraciously on the foliage. They usually cluster in colonies and attack the superficial layers of the leaf and flower so that these growths become very ragged and decay rapidly. Pupation takes place on any aquatic vegetation standing above water-level, and there may be several broods in a season.

Remedies consist of forcible spraying to dislodge them, and when fish are present there is generally little further trouble. In stockless pools, however, they must be controlled by a stomach poison such as arsenate of lead, applied in a mist-like form. Attacked plants may be forcibly submerged for several days to allow fish to clear the pest. It helps, too, to cut down the vegetation at the waterside in autumn and thus deter the beetles from hibernating there.

WATER-LILY BEETLE (*Galerucella nymphaeae*)

Another pest of local occurrence, but troublesome to eradicate. The small dark-brown beetle (about twice the size of a ladybird) hibernates during the winter in pondside vegetation and comes on the water-lilies about June. The eggs are laid in clusters on the leaf surface and hatch out in about a week. They turn into small, slug-like creatures, very dark brown above and yellowish beneath, which feed voraciously on the foliage. They usually cluster in colonies and attack the superficial layers of the leaf and flower so that these growths become very ragged and decay rapidly. Pupation takes place on any aquatic vegetation standing above water-level, and there may be several broods in a season.

Remedies consist of forcible spraying to dislodge them, and when fish are present there is generally little further trouble. In stockless pools, however, they must be controlled by a stomach poison such as arsenate of lead, applied in a mist-like form. Attacked plants may be forcibly submerged for several days to allow fish to clear the pest. It helps, too, to cut down the vegetation at the waterside in autumn and thus deter the beetles from hibernating there.

FALSE LEAF-MINING MIDGE (*Cricotopus ornatus*)
    The larvae of this pest can cause annoyance by eating narrow serpentine lines all over the leaf surface. It does not really mine into the tissues, but the general effect is the same. In fishless tanks spray with arsenate of lead or nicotine.

CADDIS FLIES (*Trichoptera*)
    Here again little trouble will be experienced by the gardener who has his pool properly stocked, for caddis fly larvae have but a short life when fish are present. The flies visit the pool in the evening, laying their eggs in or near the water. The larvae are practically all aquatic and use a conglomeration of materials, such as sticks, sand, shells and bits of plant, to make themselves a house and disguise their outline. At this stage they feed on water plants, damaging roots, flower-buds and leaves with equal indiscrimination.

Hand-picking must be resorted to in a bad infestation if no fish are present.

OTHER PESTS

Other living creatures liable at times to cause damage in the water garden are snails—especially the large pointed one known as the freshwater whelk (*Limnaea stagnalis*). In superfluous quantities it causes annoyance by devouring water lily leaves and flowers. Fish will keep it down, as they suck the slimy egg masses laid on the tank-side and leaf undersurfaces, and also devour the molluscs when young. Alternatively, a lettuce or cabbage stump laid in the tank overnight will attract vast numbers which can be shaken off and destroyed.

Larvae of dragon-flies or the *Dytiscus* water beetle are a menace to the fish fancier because of the tigerish way they attack his fish. There is no remedy but hand-picking: with particularly valuable fish it may be necessary to empty the pond to find them. They look like miniature lobsters and are every bit as fierce.

Frogs at breeding-time will also attack fish occasionally, especially if there is an 'odd man' out. It is, however, a rare occurrence, but should be borne in mind if corpses with ugly bruises on their sides are found floating in spring.

Perhaps the most ardent fish fancier of all is the domestic cat, and here the gardener must find his own remedy. Herons are even worse, and woe betide you if a heron finds your pond—even the law is on his side, for he is a protected bird. Protection can be given in a small pool with a wire-netting cover. Construct a light framework of laths and 1 or 2in plastic-covered netting and lay this over the pond in winter. It will safeguard fish from cats and birds and also give a measure of protection agains frost. A plastic-covered wire stretched along the edges 6in inside the pool deters

herons, which normally stand in the water to fish.
Mosquitoes are an obvious menace where there is stagnant water and the remedy is simple—fish!

FUNGUS DISEASES

Two leaf-spot diseases affect water-lilies, the first, due to a species of *Cerosporae*, causes the edges to dry and crumble up and spreads so rapidly that the plant soon becomes denuded of foliage. Affected leaves should be removed and the others sprayed with Bordeaux mixture at half the usual strength. A fine nozzle spray should be used and the operation repeated several times until the disease is controlled. The other leaf-spot (*Ovularia nymphaerum*) shows dark patches on the leaves which later disintegrate. A humid atmosphere encourages spreading and every affected leaf must be immediately removed.

A *Phytophthora* species can do great damage where it gets a hold, causing blackening and rotting of the stems, which may spread down to the root. The yellow forms, such as *Marliaceae chromatella* and *Moorei,* seem particularly susceptible. Affected plants must be removed and destroyed.

Appendix

PUMPS FOR WATER FEATURES

A GARDEN pool can be brought to life if water movement is introduced in the form of a fountain, waterfall or stream. The movement of water increases the oxygen content and has a certain cooling effect during very warm weather. Water features are surprisingly easy to make because the modern submersible electric pump reduces all installation work to the minimum and little or no skill is required.

It is important to appreciate the fact that the pump must circulate the water in the pool itself and no other outside source should be used The pool balance could be upset and there might be the danger of contamination.

The electric submersible type of pump is specially sealed so that the complete pump can be totally submerged in the water. No complex pipework is required and the only electrical connections needed are one to the external mains lead to the pump, and another to a conveniently situated 3-pin earthed plug in the mains supply. The connection to the pump is made outside the pool of course, and a completely weather and waterproof cable connector must be used. It is also advisable to obtain the services of a qualified electrian for all these electrical connections in the garden.

The greater the volume of water necessary, the larger the capacity of the pump must be, and the 'head' of water required will also determine choice. The head is the vertical distance between the water surface of the pool and the outlet of the pump pipe, where the water has to be pumped up to a height of several feet above the pool itself for a waterfall or stream course. Extensive pipework will increase the pressure loss and head against which the pump is working.

Quite small, cheap submersible pumps can be used in the smaller pools where the water surface area does not exceed 80sq ft. The Otter or Cub models will deliver about 330 and 250gal per hr, respectively, at a head of 3ft. For more powerful displays a submersible pump such as the Sealion C with a capacity of 1,750gal per hr at a head of some 7ft would be required. A submersible pump can be used for a fountain display quite easily because the fountain head is simply fastened to the short outlet pipe on the pump. The pump is placed on bricks in the pool so that the fountain head is just above water level. A combined fountain and waterfall can be arranged from one pump by the addition of a special tee-piece which provides a connection for the fountain head and another connection for the waterfall outlet pipe. The smaller pumps such as the Otter can be used for this purpose but only small displays can be expected and a pool not larger than 20-25sq ft in surface area should be considered. Used in combination, the output for the waterfall would be approximately 120gal per hr.

For more complex water effects, the surface type of electric pump in the 1/9th-1hp range will give an increased head and a corresponding capacity of water flow. For example, the Stuart No 25 pump is capable of delivering about 500gal per hr at a head of 35ft, and the Wade DC/25 1,270gal per hr at the same head. These large capacity pumps are ideal where several fountains are required or where a long delivery pipe has to be installed for a stream course or a waterfall.

More work is involved in installation but the use of modern polythene large bore tubing makes the work a lot easier and all the necessary bends and elbow joints etc are readily obtainable from specialist water-garden firms. The pump is housed outside the pool in its own well-ventilated housing and the pipes to and from the pump are carefully concealed. One pipe is taken into the pool where it delivers the water to the pump and other pipes are taken from the other pump connection to the various features such as fountains or waterfalls. Gate valves can be installed so that the water flow can be regulated. Filtration of the water to the pump is essential, otherwise the pump impeller could be damaged by dirt. Most of the submersible pumps have built-in strainers but the surface pumps require a separate strainer attached to the end of their inlet or suction pipe.

Index